Goldminds Publishing, LLC
P.O. Box 11109
Springfield, Missouri 65808-1109

Prairie Meals and Memories: Living the Golden Rural

Copyright © Carolyn Hall, 2008

ISBN 10: 1-930584-15-6
ISBN 13: 978-1-930584-15-0

Printed in the United States of America

Without limiting the rights under the copyright reserved above, no part of this publication may be reproduced, stored in or introduced into a retrieval system, or transmitted, in any form or by any means (electronic, mechanical, photocopying, recording or otherwise), without the prior written permission of both the copyright owner and the above publisher of this book.

www.goldmindspub.com

Prairie Meals and Memories

LIVING THE GOLDEN RURAL

By Carolyn Hall

Prairie Meals and Memories

LIVING THE GOLDEN RURAL

Carolyn (Boor) Hall grew up on a 400 acre farm in central Kansas. A sod house foundation, part of the original homestead, still lies hidden under bushes in the middle of 20 acres of virgin prairie. Her Grandfather Schreiber built the family's second home from limestone rock he hand-quarried in their pasture. The nearest town, Olmitz, a German settlement, flavored her food and her memories. She is a third generation German immigrant and learned traditions and recipes passed down through generations, modified for life on the Kansas prairie.

Carolyn's large, extended family ran a dairy, wheat farm, egg laying operation and raised turkeys, chickens, pigs, guineas and geese, but no horses—her dad had followed them behind a plow most of his early years and needed a break. For the children, the farm was an equal opportunity work force. Everyone but Grandma drove the tractors, wheat trucks and had at least one try at the combine. Carolyn learned to be self sufficient and work hard. She had the best childhood one could hope for. Her parents told her she could grow up and be anything she wanted to be as long she was willing to work for it.

Now a writer, she can be anybody, do anything, and go anywhere in her stories, but her keyboard keeps taking her back home to the little girl surrounded by the Golden Rural—wheat, sunflowers and Grandpa's yellow limestone.

She shares her love of the land, its people and heritage in *Prairie Meals and Memories*.

Dedications

For my husband John and my children Dawn, Clay and Lisa who encouraged me to write down my memories after years of my constant retelling of "Mom's stories".

To my wonderful family who helped make these stories possible, Marietta, Ronnie Lou, Loretta, Rose Mary and Johnnie and to the memory of Mom, Dad, Grandma, Uncle Frank, Marion and Gary.

To my hometown of Olmitz, Kansas, with the finest friends, hardest working farmers and the best cooks one could ever know.

Acknowledgements
Thanks to the following family and friends who contributed recipes, encouragement and fodder for my stories: Bill Armstrong, Shannon Armstrong, Ken Bardot, Jeff Boor, Johnnie Boor, Judy Boor, Rose Mary Cantrell, Tera Dooley, Ronnie Lou Drees, Mary-Lane Kamberg, Alvin Lichter, Marietta Lichter, Joy Schlochtermeier, Al Schmeidler, Theresa Schmeidler, Terri Schneider, Loretta Southard, my Friday morning critique group, and the Kansas City Writer's Group.

Introduction: Flatlanders Know How to Survive

Early settlers came to a nearly treeless landscape and learned to build houses and fences from the rock buried in their pastures. Buffalo chips and then cow pies substituted for wood in their hearths. The hard working families formed strong communities and passed their land down from generation to generation. The family farm is becoming something of a legend, just like Wyatt Earp and Wild Bill Hickock. Few can afford to live, work and raise a family on a small farm these days. Those of us fortunate enough to have lived it carry the memories and experiences close to our hearts.

Our lives revolved around farm chores, school, and monthly shopping trips. Even weddings and funerals had to be fit into the routine. We fought the weather for our crops, rebuilt after storms and carried each other through hard times. Our days started before dawn and ended with a prayer before bedtime. The fierce independence of the farmers and strong will to provide better for their children than they had in the "old country," followed by the depression forged a work ethic that formed the backbone of America.

Kiss the cook and bless the farmer...

TABLE OF CONTENTS

	Living the Golden Rural		23	Frosted Cherry Apple Pie
	Introduction		25	Red Hot Applesauce Gelatin Salad
	Part 1: Picking and Pickling		**27**	**Pickles, Jellies and Spirits**
1	"Sunbonnet Veronica"		29	"You Might Not Want That in Your Pickles"
2	Parsley Buttered Potatoes		31	Sweet & Sassy Dill Spears
3	Potato Pancakes		32	Chokecherry Jelly
4	Wilted Leaf Lettuce		33	Fresh Strawberry Freezer Syrup
5	Radish Sandwiches		35	"Eau De Sauerkraut"
6	Maple Glazed Carrots		37	Fried Sauerkraut
7	Farmer's Corn Pudding		38	Sauerkraut Dip
8	Stewed Red Cabbage		39	"Mom Spirits Are Making Noises"
9	Eggplant Fritters		40	Beet Wine
11	Green Tomato Pie		41	Hot Toddy
13	**Fruits and Salads**		**43**	**Part 2: Always Room for One More at the Table**
15	"Boone's Farm and Peaches"		45	"Dollar Days Shopping in Hoisington"
17	Winter Fruit Salad		**47**	**Breads and Breakfast**
18	Peaches 'N Cream		49	"Church Ladies and Bake Sales"
20	Mom's Pumpkin Pie		50	Olmitz Kuchen
21	Fancy Baked Apples		54	Aunt Carolyn's Carrot Cake
22	Rhubarb Crunch		56	Bohemian Poppy Seed Cake

58	"Batter Up"	95	Sloppy Joes with Beans
59	Sunflower Cake	96	Oven Barbecued Beef Brisket
62	"Four Hundred and Fifty Strokes but Who's Counting"	**99**	**Starches**
63	Brownie Sheet Cake	101	"Feed Sack Fashions"
65	"Night Life on the Farm"	103	Grandma's White Bread—Almost
69	"Son's Up, Works for Me"	105	Cake Mix Cinnamon Rolls
70	Rise and Shine Coffee Cake	107	Sweet Tooth Cornbread
71	"Prairie Know-How"	108	Sauerkraut Rye Bread
73	"Reunited For the Holidays"	110	Sunflower Oatmeal Bread
75	"He Knows if You've Been Bad or Good"	112	Old Fashioned Pie Crust
77	Chocolate Cashew Clusters	114	Cinnamon Crisps
78	Impossible Toffee Cracker Candy	115	Egg Yolk Noodles
79	Vanilla Moons	116	Noodles in Burnt Butter
81	"I Remember Mama's"	**117**	**Soups, Stews and Casseroles**
82	Christmas Stollen	119	"No Kissing Cousins, Please"
85	Apricot Filled Cookies	120	Old Fashioned Ham Bone Soup
87	"Bakery Bread And Margarine"	121	Creamy Corn Chowder
88	Mom's Chocolate Angel Food Cake	123	Al & Theresa's Green Bean and Dumpling Soup
90	Chocolate Cream Frosting	125	Rueben Soup
91	"Cattle Crossing"	127	Rye Bread Croutons
93	Prairie Oysters	129	"Did You Hear the One about ..."
94	Best Ever Meatloaf	131	Ranch Style Baked Beans

133	**Hoof, Feather and Fin**	175	"Hang 'em High"
135	"The Cows Are Out"	177	Pickled Pigs Feet
136	Sauerfleisch	179	Harvest Hand Pot Roast
138	Steak Fingers	181	Pot Roast Gravy
139	Honey Mustard Sauce	183	"Cumshawed"
140	Bierocks	185	Homemade Pizza
143	**Meat, Poultry and Fish**	187	Scaredy Cats
145	"It Takes A lot of Guts To Make Sausage"	189	Beer Battered Catfish
148	Big John's Smoked Sausage	190	Dill Dip
150	Sausage with Apples and Raisins	191	Broiled Perch in Lemon Sauce
151	Bite Size Smokies	193	Bayrischer Style Crappie
153	"Now that's Crossing the Line"	**195**	**Game**
155	Jager Schnitzel	197	"You Need a Permit for That Ma'am"
158	"Watch Where You're Steppin'"	199	Skillet Venison Leavenworth Style
159	Homemade Beef Bologna	201	Deer 'n Coke ®
161	"Fowl Play"	203	Buffalo & Beef Meatballs
163	Roast Goose	205	"Snipe Hunting in Snipes Hollow"
164	Chicken Stew	207	"Struttin' Their Stuff in the Shelterbelt"
167	"No Empty Nest"	209	Country Creamed Pheasant
169	Savory Roast Chicken	**211**	**Sweets and Treats**
171	Hot Mamas	213	"Chicken Feed and Wedding Cakes"
172	Never Fail Meringue	215	Cream Mints

216	Rosettes	241	Beer Bundt Cake
218	Soft Oatmeal Cookies	**243**	**Dairy Delights**
220	Kansas Tornado Cookies	245	"All We Have We Owe to Udders"
222	Chocolate Crinkles	247	Chocolate Delight Cream Pie
223	Peanut Butter Cyclones	248	Blueberry Ice Cream
224	Almond Lace Rings	249	Lazy Day Ice Cream
227	"Graveyard Stew"	250	Homemade Sweetened Condensed Milk
231	Haystacks	**251**	**Hand Crafted**
232	Pumpkin Bars	253	"You'll Need More than Grandma's Lye Soap to Get those Knees Clean"
234	Sunflower Seed Cookies		
235	**This and That**	255	Home Made Lye Soap
237	"In Heaven There is No Beer"	257	Depression Flower Garden
238	Red Beer	259	Cinnamon Ornaments
239	Cheesy Beer Bread	260	Play Clay

Picking and Pickling

Carolyn Hall

Sun Bonnet Veronica

Like Sun Bonnet Sue, Grandma Veronica wouldn't set foot in the garden without covering up in her home-made slat bonnet, an apron, a long sleeve shirt over her dress and a kerchief tied around her neck. Porcelain skin was a virtue to her, not the deep brown tans we got from driving the tractors in our swimsuits.

Grandma's bonnet hung from a nail just inside the front porch door. If one of the slats that held it stiff worked its way out, you could recognize part of the Kellogg's Cornflake rooster she'd cut up for her hat. To make her bonnet, she started with a good sturdy cotton feed sack, green if possible. She got her ruler and assigned one of us to cut one inch strips from the breakfast cereal box. Precision mattered—they'd better be straight and a true one inch wide and 10 inches long. The length made the bonnet extend far enough in front to keep her face in constant shadow.

Next she'd iron her fabric, measure, cut and sew the hat. She'd sew "pockets" that ran from the front of the bonnet back to where her cheekbones would be. These held the cardboard slats and made the bonnet rigid and caused it to frame her face. When she wore it, you felt as though you looked into a tunnel that led to her blue eyes.

My sisters and I rebelled against the bonnets and long sleeved shirts when we did the field work. We'd put on our swimsuits and hide them under one of Dad's oversized chambray shirts. Once safely out of Grandma's range, we'd stow the shirt in the tool box on the tractor and lather on tanning oil. No farmer's tans for us. After a little boy asked me why the front of my legs were brown and the backs white, I stood in various strange positions while I plowed to get the back of my legs tanned.

We garnered little sympathy from her when we'd scorch our backs and occasionally blistered from our sun worship. Sidebar:

Women on the prairie found many uses for their apron. It kept their dresses clean during cooking and made a good place to dry their hands. When they gathered eggs or vegetables, they'd bunch up the bottom of their apron in one hand and fill the "pouch" with the other. A good flap of an apron shooed flies off an apple pie cooling on the front porch and a shy child could disappear behind it when a visitor came by.

Parsley Buttered Potatoes

Fast and easy side dish. Russet, Yukon Gold or new potatoes work well. Serve with meatloaf, green beans and cinnamon applesauce.
Serves 4

Ingredients:

- 4 medium potatoes, peeled and quartered
- Water to cook
- ½ teaspoon salt
- ¼ cup butter or margarine, melted
- 1 tablespoon dried parsley flakes
- ½ tablespoon dried chopped chives
- Salt and pepper to taste

Directions:

1. Place potatoes in saucepan. Add water just to cover potatoes. Sprinkle with ½ teaspoon salt. Place lid on pan and bring to boil. Reduce heat and simmer 20 minutes or until fork tender. Drain.
2. Add butter, parsley, chives, and salt and pepper. Toss gently.

Prairie Superstition
Potatoes planted on St. Patrick's Day will yield a bumper crop.

Potato Pancakes

You can't go wrong with this side dish. You can partner it up with bacon and eggs for breakfast, smoked sausage and sauerkraut for lunch or oven baked pork chops for supper. Just add a little applesauce on top of the spud cakes for maximum enjoyment.
Serves 12—depending on size of pancakes desired

Ingredients:
- 4 medium russet potatoes, scrubbed
- ¼ cup minced onion
- 1 tablespoon flour
- 1 egg, beaten
- 1 teaspoon salt
- ½ teaspoon pepper
- oil for frying

Directions:
1. Shred potatoes into bowl. Squeeze and drain off excess liquid.
2. Add onion, flour, egg, salt and pepper and toss to blend well.
3. Coat bottom of large skillet with oil. Heat.
4. Drop spoonfuls of mixture into skillet. Flatten into thin circles with a spatula.
5. Fry until brown over medium heat. Turn and cook until potatoes are tender and browned on both sides.

Lunch or dinner? Dinner or supper? At our table, we had lunch Monday through Saturday and it turned into dinner on Sunday on special occasions. As for dinner in the evening, we fixed supper every day of the week.

Wilted Leaf Lettuce

A sweet and sour delight made from garden fresh lettuce. Grandma poured any excess bacon grease into her bacon jar on the stove to use for frying potatoes later. For a modern version, substitute olive oil for the bacon grease and add a few drops of Liquid Smoke ® to replace bacon flavor. Remove any large stems and garden critters from the lettuce, wash and drain.
Serves 4-6 servings

Ingredients:
- 1 large bowl tender lettuce leaves
- 4-6 strips of bacon
- ¼ cup cider vinegar
- ¼ cup sugar
- 2 hard boiled eggs, peeled and chopped, optional
- salt and pepper to taste

Directions:
1. Tear lettuce into large pieces. Toss with hard boiled eggs. Set aside.
2. Fry bacon in skillet until crisp. Remove bacon. Cool and crumble.
3. Combine bacon drippings (¼ cup), vinegar, sugar, salt and pepper. Bring to boil.
4. Immediately, pour over lettuce mixture and toss. Top with bacon crumbles.

Prairie Tip
Grandma put her tiny Black Seeded Simpson lettuce seeds in a saltshaker to plant.

Radish Sandwiches

We couldn't wait till Grandma pulled up the first bunch of radishes from the garden. These taste best before the radishes turn strong from the heat of summer.
Makes 1 open-faced sandwich

Ingredients:
- 2-3 fresh radishes, sliced thin
- 1 slice white bread
- butter or margarine
- salt to taste

Directions:
1. Butter bread. Arrange radish slices on top of bread. Salt. Enjoy.

Prairie Folklore
Apply a mixture of melted white wax, honey and the juice of lilies to the face to remove wrinkles.

Maple Glazed Carrots

A tasty way to get your vitamin A for the day. You can microwave this recipe with good results. Follow your microwave's directions for cooking fresh vegetables. Add the butter, cinnamon and syrup and microwave an additional 30 seconds. Stir to melt the butter.
Serves 6

Ingredients:
- 1 pound baby carrots
- ½ cup maple syrup
- ¼ cup butter or margarine
- ½ teaspoon cinnamon
- salt to taste
- water to cover

Directions:
1. Cover carrots with water, salt to taste. Bring to boil and simmer 10 minutes or until crisp tender. Drain.
2. Add butter, cinnamon and syrup. Cook over medium heat about 10 minutes, stirring often.

Prairie Superstition
A foggy day in January brings frost in May

Farmer's Corn Pudding

Instead of cornbread, try this with barbecued ribs, wilted lettuce salad and watermelon fresh from the creek patch. I use the Jiffy cornbread mix. You can add finely chopped red pepper and green onions for a bit of a kick.
Serves 8 to 10

Ingredients:
- ½ cup butter or margarine, melted
- 1 egg, beaten
- 1 cup sour cream
- 1 small box cornbread mix, 8.5 ounce size
- 1 can creamed corn
- 1 can whole kernel corn, drained

Directions:
1. Preheat oven to 350°.
2. Mix all ingredients together, just until blended. Pour into greased 9" square pan.
3. Bake 55-60 minutes.

Stewed Red Cabbage

An eye catching side dish that livens up any meal. You can substitute red wine for the apple juice, but add 2 sliced apples during cooking if you do.

Serves: 8

Ingredients:
- 1 medium head red cabbage, finely sliced
- 1 large onion, chopped
- 1 bay leaf
- salt and pepper to taste
- dash ground cloves
- dash nutmeg
- ¼ teaspoon cinnamon
- 2 cups apple juice

Directions:
1. Add cabbage and onion to stock pot. Add bay leaf and spices.
2. Pour apple juice over cabbage. Cover and simmer 1½-2 hours.

Prairie Folklore
To cure a canker sore, apply the ashes from a burnt corncob several times a day.

Eggplant Fritters

After you've tried that pretty vegetable in the seed catalog, you wonder what to do with it when you have a dozen in your root cellar. This recipe will take care of that problem. I peel, cube and freeze the eggplant for fritters year round. Serve for brunch or as a side with baked ham. They freeze and reheat well.
Makes 1 dozen depending on size

Ingredients:
- 1 medium eggplant, peeled and chunked
- 1½ cups flour
- 1 cup milk
- ½ cup sugar
- 2 eggs, separated
- 1 teaspoon baking powder

Topping:
½ cup powdered sugar

Directions:
1. Place eggplant in saucepan, cover with water. Bring to boil and simmer till soft, about 15 minutes. Drain, mash and cool.
2. Beat egg whites until stiff. Set aside.
3. Mix flour, sugar and baking powder in bowl.
4. Whisk egg yolks and combine with milk and eggplant. Pour into dry mixture. Stir until well blended. Fold in egg whites.
5. Pour about ¼ cup batter on hot, lightly greased griddle or heavy skillet. Cook until golden brown on both sides. Sprinkle with powdered sugar, serve warm.

Home Grown Freezer Spaghetti Sauce

A good way to use your less than perfect homegrown tomatoes and enjoy them throughout the winter months. Just add ground beef, meatballs or sausage and serve over cooked spaghetti noodles. Top with grated Parmesan cheese.

Makes 5 pints

Ingredients:
- ¼ bushel or about 45 medium tomatoes
- 6 garlic cloves, minced
- 3 large onions, chopped
- ½ cup fresh parsley, chopped fine
- ¼ cup brown sugar, packed
- 2 tablespoons salt, non-iodized
- 1 tablespoon oregano
- 1½ tablespoons basil
- ½ teaspoon pepper

Directions:
1. Cut stem ends from tomatoes and cut in large chunks. Place in large stockpot and bring to boil. Stir frequently.
2. Reduce heat, cover and simmer 15-20 minutes until tomatoes are soft. Stir occasionally. Cool.
3. Process in blender or food processor until juicy but not pureed.
4. Press through coarse sieve or food mill. Discard skin and seeds.
5. Return tomato paste to stockpot and add garlic, onion, parsley, brown sugar, and spices. Bring to boil. Reduce heat and simmer uncovered 4 hours or until sauce reaches desired consistency. Stir occasionally.
6. Cool sauce. Ladle into freezer containers, leaving 1 inch headspace, or seal in freezer bags.

Green Tomato Pie

Mom couldn't let anything go to waste. Just before she'd pull up the tomato plants in the fall, she'd gather one last harvest of green tomatoes. This recipe finished off the last of them. Use Old Fashioned Pie Crust recipe page 112.
Serves 8

Ingredients:
- 1 pastry recipe 9" double crust pie
- 3 cups green tomatoes, sliced thin
- 1⅓ cups sugar
- 3 tablespoons flour
- 1 teaspoon cinnamon
- ½ teaspoon nutmeg
- ¼ teaspoon salt
- dash of ground cloves
- 4 tablespoon grated lemon rind
- 6 tablespoons fresh lemon juice
- 3 tablespoons butter or margarine

Directions:
1. Preheat oven to 450°. Line 9" pie pan with half the pie dough.
2. In large bowl, combine tomatoes, sugar, flour, spices, water, lemon juice and lemon rind. Toss lightly to coat tomato slices.
3. Pour into pastry shell. Dot with butter. Cover with remaining pastry dough. Cut slits to vent top crust.
4. Bake for 10 minutes at 450°. Reduce heat to 350° continue baking for 30 minutes or until done.

 **Prairie Tip**
To ripen green tomatoes, place in a brown paper bag and store in a cool dry place for several days. Check often. Mom sent a sack of green tomatoes to college with me to bake this pie. Once back at school, I forgot about the pie for almost a week. We enjoyed sliced ripe tomatoes instead.

Carolyn Hall

Fruits and Salads

Prairie Meals & Memories: Living the Golden Rural

Boone's Farm and Peaches

"Mae said the peaches at Glantz Gardens are the best ever this year," Mom announced, hanging up the telephone. "Why don't you and your dad go pick me a half a bushel before lunch?"

"Sounds good to me," I said. With just a few days left until college started at K-State, this would give me a chance to have an outing with Dad. He worked as a roughneck in the oilfields seven days a week to support his farming habit. Today was a rare day off because they were moving the oil rig to a new location.

"It's gonna be a scorcher," Dad said. "We'd better get going before it gets any hotter."

In Kansas, a cloudless August day heats up fast. I remembered the suntan lotion, but left the ice water on the kitchen counter. Halfway to the produce farm, I realized we'd left our drink at home.

We stopped by a friend of Dad's on the way. He ran a liquor store that also sold pop. My drink of choice was Dr. Pepper. I was the teetotaler of the family but Dad, a full-blooded German, preferred beer. The pop delivery hadn't arrived so we had only two choices of cold drinks from his cooler, beer or Boone's Farm Strawberry Wine. I may have been born German, but I couldn't stand the taste of beer, so bless Dad's kind heart, he bought a couple of bottles of the strawberry wine to take with us.

"I think you'll like the taste of this," Dad said.

By the time we got to Glantz's farm and got a ride to the peach orchard on the trailer attached to his tractor, the mercury had risen to 104°.

We hopped off the back and thanked him for the ride.

"I'll just leave the tractor here. Come get me when you've picked all you want," the driver said. "Just line 'em up in the wagon, I'll get 'em to your truck. Feel free to sample the fruit. Best crop we've had in years."

I'd skipped breakfast, so the thought of one of those huge peaches sounded inviting. I plucked one from the branch and took a bite. Sheer bliss. The hot golden fruit tasted like a peach cobbler. I shared it with Dad.

"I think your mom would like a full bushel of these," he said.

We scanned the rows of petite trees loaded with the golden nuggets. A dry wind blew through the orchard. Dad opened the first bottle of wine.

"This isn't bad," I said. "And it's nice and cold."

Dad brought a basket over to the tree we'd selected. "We can fill the whole thing from this tree."

We picked the bushel and finished the first bottle. Small peach trees have little shade value and the sun inched higher in the sky.

"You anxious for school to start?" he asked.

"Once I get back in the routine, it won't be bad." My mouth felt prickly and dust stuck to the peach juice on my cheek. I opened the second bottle of wine. "Would you look at that tree over there? We missed the best ones."

"I'll get another basket." Dad said. "You must like that wine."

I looked down, I'd finished half of it. It tasted like strawberry pop and went down easy. Must not be very potent, I thought.

Dad took his red handkerchief from his pocket and mopped the streams of sweat on his forehead. I passed him the last of the Boone's Farm.

We talked and picked and talked and picked. The driver came to check on us.

"Started to worry. It shouldn't take that long to pick a bushel or two," he said and looked at our baskets. "Guess you needed a few more than you thought."

Dad helped him load the peaches and we walked back to the barn to settle our bill. We then put the fruit in our pickup bed and headed for home.

"How many were we supposed to get?" Dad asked.

"A bushel or two I think," I said.

The old Chevy had no air conditioning, so we rode with the windows down. The dry summer air made me drowsy. The next thing I knew, we were home and Dad pulled up under the shade tree in front of the house. Mom came out to greet us and saw the load in the truck.

"What army did you bring all these for?"

"They're the best he's had in years," Dad said.

"We figured you'd want a few more once you knew how good they were." I said, waking up.

"How many would a few be?" She asked.

Dad grinned and looked at me, "I guess five bushel, if I counted right."

Mom went back inside and returned with two paring knives. "You picked 'em, you can 'em."

And we did, all afternoon and into the evening. They're still the best peaches I've ever tasted. As for the Boone's Farm, I learned to stick to Dr. Pepper.

Prairie Superstition
When the Big Dipper pours into the Little Dipper it spills over and rain will fall.

Winter Fruit Salad

Revisit wonderful summer peaches anytime with this simple mixture. Any variety of apple works, I prefer a bright red variety to add extra color on a dreary cold day.
Serves 6

Ingredients:
- 2 cups sliced canned peaches and juice (about 16 ounces)
- 1 banana, sliced
- 1 apple, sliced
- sugar (optional)
- ¼ cup chopped pecans (optional)
- 1 teaspoon apple pie spice or ½ teaspoon nutmeg and ½ cinnamon

Directions:
1. Mix fruit in bowl. Sprinkle spice over fruit and toss.
2. Sweeten to taste if needed. Add nuts if desired.

Seed catalogs filled our mailbox in late winter. Grandma studied them and planned her garden and consulted the almanac for proper planting times.

Peaches 'N Cream

The canned peaches in this recipe let you bring back the sweet taste of summertime any season of the year. Serves 6 to 8

Ingredients:
- ¾ cup flour
- 1 teaspoon baking powder
- ½ teaspoon salt
- 1 package vanilla pudding mix (not instant)
- 3 tablespoons butter or margarine
- 1 egg
- ½ cup milk
- 1 28-ounce can peaches, drain, reserve syrup
- 1 8-ounce package cream cheese
- ½ cup sugar
- 3 to 4 tablespoons reserved peach syrup

Topping:
- 1 tablespoon sugar
- ½ teaspoon cinnamon

Directions:
1. Preheat oven to 350°.
2. Combine flour, baking powder, salt, pudding, butter, egg and milk. Beat 2 minutes on medium speed. Pour batter into well greased 10" deep dish pie plate.
3. Arrange peaches on top of batter.

4. Combine cream cheese, sugar and reserved peach syrup. Beat until smooth. This should be thick but spreadable, add more syrup as needed. Pour onto peaches. Spread to within 1" of sides of pan.
5. Mix cinnamon and sugar for topping and sprinkle on cream cheese mixture. Bake 30-35 minutes. Chill before serving.

Most cars didn't have air conditioning. We had 4/40 air conditioning instead—4 windows down at 40 miles an hour.

Roughneck is slang for an oilfield worker. They worked on the derrick, a tall tower used to support the drilling apparatus. A lot of farmers in Kansas and Oklahoma took jobs as roughnecks when the farm economy didn't pay enough to cover the bills. Their commute took almost two hours each way. They'd work the 3 pm-11 pm shift to leave their mornings free to do their fieldwork.

Mom's Pumpkin Pie
Thanksgiving wouldn't be the same without it. This is quick and easy which helps with busy holidays. Use Old Fashioned Pie Crust recipe page 112.
Serves 8

Ingredients:
- 2 cups pumpkin (15 to 16 ounce can)
- 1 14-ounce can sweetened condensed milk
- 1 egg, beaten
- ½ teaspoon salt
- ½ teaspoon nutmeg
- ½ teaspoon ginger
- ½ teaspoon pumpkin pie spice
- 1 teaspoon cinnamon
- 1 unbaked 9" pie shell

Directions:
1. Preheat oven to 375°.
2. Mix all ingredients together. (I like to use a food processor for a smoother filling). Pour into pie shell.
3. Bake 50-55 minutes. Cool. Refrigerate at least 1 hour before serving.

Farmers dug root cellars into the ground, lined them with limestone and covered them with sod. Grandpa dug ours just off the porch with a covered access. We filled bins in the cellar with potatoes, beets, carrots, cabbage and onions. Mom stored her canned goods and Grandma kept her eggs down there. It never froze in winter and stayed cool enough in summer to chill a watermelon.

Fancy Baked Apples

This side dish dresses up any meal. Add a dollop of whipped cream and you've also got a quick dessert. Tart apples work well, but you can use any kind you have on hand. No need to peel the apples. You can substitute 1½ teaspoons apple pie spice for the spices.
Serves 4

Ingredients:
- 2 apples, sliced or chopped
- 1 tablespoon raisins
- 1 tablespoon craisins
- ¼ cup walnuts, chopped
- 1 teaspoon cinnamon
- ½ teaspoon nutmeg
- dash allspice
- 2 tablespoons brown sugar
- 1 tablespoon water

Directions:
1. Preheat oven to 350º.
2. Add all ingredients to a casserole dish, cover.
3. Microwave on high 4 minutes or bake 20 minutes or until fork tender.

Prairie Superstition
If a crescent moon lies horizontal in the sky, a dry spell's coming.

Rhubarb Crunch

Sweet and simple, be sure and serve this hot, and top off with a scoop of vanilla ice cream. If you're in a hurry, microwave the rhubarb mixture 7 minutes on high, stirring twice during cooking time. Add topping and microwave another 7 minutes.
Serves 8-10

Ingredients:
- 4 cups rhubarb, diced
- 1 cup sugar
- 3 tablespoons flour
- 1 cup brown sugar
- 1½ cups flour
- 1 cup oatmeal
- 1 cup margarine

Directions:
1. Preheat oven to 375°.
2. Mix rhubarb, 1 cup sugar and 3 tablespoons flour together and place in 6"x10" greased baking dish.
3. Combine brown sugar, 1½ cups flour and oatmeal. Cut in margarine until mixture crumbles between fingers. Sprinkle over rhubarb mixture.
4. Bake 40 minutes.

Frosted Cherry Apple Pie

If you can't decide which is your favorite flavor of pie, this one gives you the best of both. Use Old Fashioned Pie Crust recipe page 112.
Serves 8

Ingredients:
- 2 unbaked pie crusts
- 1 21-ounce can cherry pie filling
- 5 cups apples, sliced with peels
- ½ cup sugar
- ½ cup brown sugar
- 4 tablespoons flour
- 1 teaspoon cinnamon
- 1 teaspoon nutmeg
- 1 teaspoon apple pie spice
- 4 teaspoons butter or margarine

Frosting:
½ cup powdered sugar
¼ teaspoon vanilla
2 teaspoons milk (enough to make a smooth paste)

Directions:
1. Preheat oven to 400°.
2. Line deep dish pie pan with 1 crust.
3. In large bowl, mix flour, sugars and spices. Add apple slices and toss to coat.
4. Pour into prepared pie shell. Dot with butter. Spoon cherry pie filling over top of apple mixture.

5. Cover with top crust, cut vent slices in dough. Cover edge of pie with foil and bake 25 minutes. Remove foil and bake 25-30 minutes more.
6. Remove from oven. Top with frosting.

Frosting: Stir powdered sugar, vanilla and milk until smooth and slightly thick. Spread on top of pie. Serve warm.

Red Hot Applesauce Gelatin Salad

This molded salad adds a touch of color and zest to your meal. Use small, individual heart-shaped molds or one large heart mold as a centerpiece for Valentine's Day. If you prefer less cinnamon flavor, reduce red hots to ¼ cup.
Serves 4-6

Ingredients:
- 1 cup boiling water
- 1 3-ounce package cherry gelatin
- ⅓ cup red hot candies
- 1 cup applesauce, chilled

Directions:
1. Bring water and red hots to boil. Add gelatin and stir until dissolved.
2. Add applesauce, stirring well.
3. Pour into molds or serving dish and chill.

Prairie Meals & Memories: Living the Golden Rural

Carolyn Hall

Pickles, Jellies and Spirits

Prairie Meals & Memories: Living the Golden Rural

Carolyn Hall

You Might Not Want That in Your Pickles

Grandma's garden produced a bounty of cucumbers. What we didn't eat fresh in salads, Mom pickled. Bread and butter, dills of every shape and size and even sweet red cinnamon slices that rivaled candied apples. After she'd tried every familiar recipe, she turned to one clipped from the local paper.

"Grape leaves, that's new." She said. "Gives an interesting flavor to your dills," she read aloud from the article.

"Where you gonna get grape leaves?" I asked.

"Snipes Hollow. They grow wild and vine on the red cedars next to Reimer's pasture," she said and smiled at me. "Want to take a grocery sack and pick some?"

She knew I loved to walk the dirt path that led to the twenty acres of virgin prairie, our hay ground we called Snipes Hollow. We grazed the dairy cows in the pasture next to it during summer and early fall afternoons before the evening milking. At ten years old, I'd herded the cows there and back many times.

I put on my shoes and grabbed the sack from her hands.

"Be sure and pick them from the west side of the tree." Mom hollered after me.

I skipped and sang while my shoes kicked up warm dust on the road between the barn corral and the field full of wheat stubble awaiting the plow. The tire-rutted road wound past the smaller pasture close to home and the four-strand barbed wire fence stretched between stone posts.

An occasional extra long road thorn lodged in the bottom of my shoe and stuck into my foot. I'd hop over to a limestone fence post and rake the thorn against the post rock until the sticker dislodged. The activity started a prairie dog barking from one of the hundreds of mounds sprinkled throughout the pasture. His warning spread and a chorus of shrill barks filled the summer quiet and I moved to the far side of the path. I kept my distance whenever possible from the critters.

On several occasions, my older sister Rose and her friend Joy had threatened to tie my brother and me together and set us over a prairie dog hole. We delighted in pestering the girls, but when they'd lose patience with our tag-along antics, they'd do their best to shake our company.

"They like kids the best." They'd say. "Hear them bark? They're talking about lunch already."

That stopped us in our tracks. Mom promised those little varmints wouldn't hurt me, but I didn't trust them anymore.

The prairie dogs decided I wasn't a threat and retreated into their tunnels. I continued on my errand and walked past the gaping hole in the side of a rise next to the pasture. The trench silo waited to be filled with this year's corn crop. I teetered along the edge, putting one foot in front of the other and walked an imaginary tightrope, with arms stretched out wide. A faint sour smell still lingered from last year's silage.

At the end of the silo, my foot brushed a clump of grass and scared up a meadowlark. I screamed and she scolded me on her way skyward. I broke into a run and didn't stop until I reached the edge of the hay ground.

All that running made me thirsty. I spied the big juicy chokecherries growing in the fence line. You had to be careful and only eat the darkest ones or you'd be puckered for a week. Mom would be glad to know they were ripe. We could bring a bucket later when we came to get the cows. She made the best choke cherry jelly. I wiped my purple stained hands on the front of my shorts and headed toward the red cedars.

But I stopped first and walked the tops of the stones half buried in the dirt, an old foundation in the center of the hay ground. This small rectangle, the size of the living room of our farmhouse, held the base of the sod house my great-grandfather built on this land he homesteaded. I couldn't imagine growing up in a house so tiny. My brother and I would've killed each other.

The wind picked up. I spun around and around in the tall grass, letting the paper sack billow in the breeze. I collapsed on the ground and studied the cedar tree.

Where did Mom say the vines grew? The west side? But I didn't know which was the west side. Mom couldn't keep track which of us knew our directions. There were different vines growing on two sides of the tree. I decided to fill the bag with the ones that had small berries on them. That must be what wild grapes look like.

On my tip toes, I reached up and got the biggest leaves clinging to the green boughs and the Christmas tree smell filled my nose while I pulled the leafy vines loose.

With my sack full, I headed for home, satisfied I'd done a good job. When I opened the kitchen door and presented my gatherings to mom, she shuddered.

"What's the matter?" I asked holding up a handful of the green foliage.

"Sweetheart, you didn't get grape leaves. You've picked a sack of poison ivy." She said shaking her head.

Mom's pickles did without the grape leaves, and luckily I did without calamine lotion.

Folklore
Jesse James and his brother, Frank, stopped in Snipes Hollow to water their horses while our neighbor watched from the safety of the bushes.

Sweet & Sassy Dill Spears

Try this upgrade on old fashioned dill pickles, sweet with a kick. They're barbecued rib's new best friend. Be careful, you can't stop with one. When you've eaten all the pickles, add a dozen hard boiled eggs to the jar. You'll get double duty from your brine—be sure and give them 4 days to absorb the flavor.

Makes 1 gallon

Ingredients:
- 1 gallon whole dill pickles
- 8 cups sugar (4 pounds)
- 6 ounces Louisiana Hot Sauce

Directions:
1. Drain juice from pickles and reserve. Slice pickles into spears.
2. Repack spears into gallon jar. Add sugar and hot sauce. Top off the jar with the reserved brine.
3. Screw lid on tightly. Store in refrigerator. Turn jar upside down every other day for 4 days. (I stand it in a pan when it's upside down to guard against drips.)

In late summer, Dad "filled silo" with the help of neighbors. They augured green chopped corn into an upright silo, the tall cylinders still seen along many highways and interstates today. He'd also fill our trench silo, a deep hole dug into the side of a small hill. The silage fermented and provided cattle feed in the winter months when grass wasn't available.

Chokecherry Jelly

We called them chokecherry bushes, some call them trees, either way they made the best jelly with a very distinctive flavor, a pioneer favorite. They grew wild in the fencerows along our native prairie hay ground. Every year we raced the birds to the ripe fruit. Wash the chokecherries, cover with water and heat gently 15 minutes or until juice starts to flow from fruit. Press lightly through a jelly bag or double layer of cheesecloth. One pound of fruit yields about 1 cup juice.

Makes 5-6 half pints

Ingredients:
- 3½ cups chokecherry juice
- 4 cups sugar
- 1 box powdered pectin

Directions:
1. Pour juice into large saucepan. Stir in pectin. Bring to boil over high heat, stirring constantly.
2. Add sugar then boil hard 1 minute, stirring constantly.
3. Remove from heat and skim off any foam. Follow pectin package directions for sealing jelly in jars.

If you've ever eaten a chokecherry before it's ripe, you'll understand how it got its name.

Fresh Strawberry Freezer Syrup

I made freezer jam for years, and decided to add more fruit. It resulted in a thinner consistency and a stronger strawberry flavor. It's incredibly easy. Mash the fruit by hand, not in the blender or processor, it leaves more uniform chunks of strawberries. Try it over waffles, pancakes or ice cream.
Makes about 4 pints

Ingredients:
- 5 cups strawberries, caps removed and quartered
- 3 cups sugar
- 1 box powdered fruit pectin
- ¾ cup water

Directions:
1. Mash fruit in baking pan, one layer at a time. (a pastry blender works well). Pour into large bowl.
2. Add sugar and mix well. Let set 10 minutes.
3. In small saucepan, add water and stir in pectin. Heat to full boil. Stir continuously and boil 1 minute.
4. Pour immediately into fruit and stir continually for 3 minutes. Ladle into jars, leaving ½" head space. Wipe rims of jars (prevents sticking when opening). Screw on tight fitting lids.
5. Let stand at room temperature 24 hours. Freeze. Keep refrigerated after opening.

Trees were in short supply on the prairie. Farmers learned to hand quarry 10-12 foot long honey-colored limestone fence posts. They sank them in the ground 4-5 feet and strung barbed wire between them to contain their cattle. They lasted over 100 years and many can still be seen along roadsides in the farm country of Central Kansas.

Prairie Meals & Memories: Living the Golden Rural

Eau De Sauerkraut

In October every year, Dad ordered a bulk load of fresh cabbage from the local IGA. When it arrived, he'd go five miles away to the Otis train depot, and pick up several 80 pound gunny sacks of the freshly harvested vegetable. Grandma retrieved the "slaw cutter" from storage and Mom cleaned the three-foot tall crocks used to cure sauerkraut. When our family sat eleven around the dinner table, we filled several crocks with the salt cured kraut for the next year's larder.

Everyone took a turn shredding the cabbage on a large mandolin style wooden slicer, the size of a scrub board. A small wooden box attached to the top held the cabbage head in place while strained arm muscles pulled it back and forth over the blades. Mom chopped the heads in half and removed the cores while Grandma kept a watchful eye on the novice helpers.

"You'll take your finger off if you're not paying attention." She'd warn when our mouths moved faster than our hands, and we'd let our fingers get too near the metal cutters.

When the top of the head had about an inch left above the blade, she tossed it into a large white enamel dishpan. Later, her practiced fingers worked these 'heels' through the cutter without a nick or scrape—the benefit of decades of practice.

We filled buckets of the fresh kraut and with the family bucket brigade we lowered them into a small cinder block basement that came with the addition of indoor plumbing. With no stairs, we climbed down a ladder to access the large crocks Dad moved to the basement. He added layers of shredded cabbage alternately with handfuls of pickling salt. My brother and I, the youngest and smallest shoe size in the family, sat on the side of the crocks while a big sister rolled up our jeans and scoured our feet. We swung our feet into the cool cabbage and stomped the salt into the shreddings until our toes squished in brine.

I stood nearly chest deep in the empty crock and enjoyed the feeling of growing out of the crock as each new layer elevated me higher.

"Mix, don't pulverize," Mom reminded us on a visit to check our progress when she caught my brother and I in a race in place in our crocks.

When we reached the top, our feet would sink knee deep and make a "lurrrp" noise when we pulled out each foot. This slowed our pace and zapped our energy. I liked to pretend I had fallen into quicksand and struggled for my life. This drama went unnoticed by whichever big sister had been assigned as spotter to keep us from falling over the side of the crock. Eventually, a baseball bat replaced little feet packing and pressing the cabbage.

The hot water heater for the house occupied a corner of the 8 ft x 10 ft basement, making it the warmest place in the house in cold weather. With the last of the cabbage/salt added and incorporated, Mom placed a large plate in each crock, sat a gallon glass jug of water on top to weight it down, and covered them with a white tea towel. She monitored it daily. When the taste and texture reached its peak, she canned it in quart jars and moved them to the root cellar.

As family members grew up and moved away, the process relocated upstairs to a lone, shorter crock in the corner of the kitchen near the wall furnace. A large wooden potato masher, handcrafted by my brother, worked well in the smaller crock. With the water jar and tea towel added, the contraption looked like a ghost in residence just in time for Halloween. As it cured, the blower on the furnace spread the distinct aroma through out the house.

Cooked, cold or combined in a recipe, there's nothing like homemade sauerkraut.

Fried Sauerkraut

Nothing goes better with smoked sausage or brats than this side dish. Grandma used to dip into her bacon grease jar to make it, but I use margarine.
Serves 4-5

Ingredients:
½ cup onion, chopped fine
2 tablespoons butter or margarine
2 tablespoons flour
1 can sauerkraut, drained, reserve liquid
1 teaspoon caraway seed

Directions:
1. In skillet, sauté onion in butter over medium heat. Stir in flour until well blended and slightly browned. Add reserved liquid from sauerkraut. Continue stirring until thickened and bubbly. (If necessary, add small amount of water). Cook and stir 1 to 2 minutes more.
2. Blend in sauerkraut and caraway seed. Cook and stir until heated through. Serve hot.

Sauerkraut Dip

Serve this warm with corn chips or cocktail rye bread for your next get-together. A slow cooker works well for this recipe.
Makes 3½-4 cups

Ingredients:
- ½ pound hamburger or sausage
- ½ cup chopped onion
- ¼ cup chopped green pepper
- 8 ounces sour cream
- 1 small can sauerkraut (about 8 ounces)
- 1 medium tomato, chopped
- 4 ounces cream cheese
- ½ teaspoon pepper
- 1 teaspoon garlic powder

Directions:
1. Brown hamburger, onion and green pepper in large skillet. Drain.
2. Blend in remaining ingredients. Simmer over low heat, stirring often until well blended and thickened.
3. For slow cooker, blend as above and simmer on low 3-4 hours, stirring occasionally.

Carolyn Hall

Mom Spirits Are Making Noises

Grandma had raised a bumper crop of beets that year. She and Mom exhausted every conceivable way to cook or can them—or so I thought. One night during supper, I kept hearing strange noises, a muted glub from under the table.

Mom said nothing but her face told the story. It started with a chuckle that grew to a giggle.

"I'll start the dishes," she said and got up and turned her back on us. I looked under the table and saw a large brown crock. It had been there for over a week, but I assumed it had been brought up to make sauerkraut and had been stored under the table.

"Don't disturb it." Mom said over her shoulder. She had 20-20 rear view vision.

"What is 'it'?" My brother asked.

"My nine day wine." She said shaking from laughter.

"Wine?" I asked. Mom didn't like alcohol. "Why are you making wine?"

"I found a recipe in the paper and thought I'd use up some of the beets."

"Beet wine?" My brother said, his brows lost in the furrows of his forehead.

"You won't be drinking it so don't worry about it."

Once she'd said it had beets in it, she knew that's one recipe I wouldn't taste. The crock disappeared in the next few days and so did the wine. Dad had fun distributing it to the neighbors and mom retired as winemaker.

Beet Wine

This goes from beets to wine in a very short time, but make sure you let it ferment a full nine days for the best results.
Makes 1 gallon

Ingredients:
- 10 medium beets, peeled and quartered
- 1 gallon water
- 6 cups sugar
- 3 lemons, sliced
- 6 cups raisins
- 1 cake yeast
- 1 slice bread, toasted hard

Directions:
1. Place beets in large pot. Cover with the water and bring to boil. Cook until tender, not mushy.
2. Remove beets. Add enough water to make a full gallon.
3. Pour into crock or dark jar (can cover outside of clear glass with brown paper).
4. Add sugar, raisins, and sliced lemons. Stir until sugar dissolves.
5. Spread yeast onto toast. Lay on top of liquid. Store in dark place at room temperature.
6. Do not stir again. Let ferment 9 full days.
7. Strain through cloth. Bottle but do not cork tightly

Hot Toddy

Soar throat? Stomach malady? Over did it outside? Mom's hot toddy was just the thing to cure what ailed you.
Serves 1

Ingredients:
- ¼ cup bourbon (some conditions may require more)
- ¾ cup boiling-hot water
- 2 heaping teaspoons sugar (may substitute honey)

Directions:
1. Add bourbon to hot water. Stir in sugar until dissolved.
2. Go to bed early if you can.

I didn't qualify for a hot toddy. Instead, I got rubbed down from chin to ribs with vapor rub. Then Mom warmed a tea towel by holding it over a low flame on the gas stove top, wrapped it around my neck and fastened it snug with a silver safety pin. I don't know how medicinal the warmed towel was, but it sure felt good.

Prairie Meals & Memories: Living the Golden Rural

Carolyn Hall

Always Room for One More at the Table

Prairie Meals & Memories: Living the Golden Rural

Carolyn Hall

Dollar Days Shopping in Hoisington

As a young girl I was raised on a farm near Olmitz, population 150. Our monthly eight-mile trips to Hoisington, were exciting excursions to the big city of 3000.

Our trips to town were strategically planned around Dollar Days, the first Wednesday of the month. Mom and Grandma would pore over the Dollar Days Shopper in the Hoisington Dispatch. Mom made the list for Mammels grocery while Grandma did the same for Town and Country. We had to make egg deliveries to Doc McGill's wife on Main, and a stop by Dr. Adkins for his special tonic for Grandma.

School shopping was something special. Instead of taking the side streets to avoid the sale day traffic, we'd head downtown. I loved the noise of the tires as they rumbled along the brick paved streets.

We'd park in front of Brown McDonald's dry goods store. The textured metal ceiling, which I imagined as an oversized satin quilt, was full of the most curious contraptions. There were the suspended spools of string, which were used to neatly tie up the brown paper wrappings that securely held your purchases, and those wonderful tubes that whooshed from the counter to that mysterious person secreted somewhere in the ceiling who sent down your change.

Next, we'd head down the block for shoes from Buster Brown. My brother and I would race to see who would be first to use that magical machine that measured how much your feet had grown. We'd sit down to try on our Poll Parrot Shoes. Then on to Duckwalls to purchase school supplies: 32 crayons, pencils, eraser, ruler, a jar of paste, and one Big Chief tablet.

Outside, the aroma of fresh doughnuts from Tindall's Bakery would overcome us. We always took home a sack of those delights as a treat. Our mouths watered as we entered through an oversized screen door that bounced shut behind us. We'd all pick our favorites—mine was the maple crème frosting with chopped nuts and I'd proudly carry the bulging white paper sack with the grease stains to the car—holding it away from my good dress as Mom directed.

On extra warm days, Mom could be persuaded to stop by the Rexall soda fountain and we'd get cherry colas to drink on the way home. The trick was to finish the drink before the round white cardboard carton got so saturated that your drink tasted more of cardboard than cola.

The car loaded and errands done, we'd head back home. I was usually asleep by the time we crossed Blood Creek outside of Hoisington. Once home we'd have to change and do the chores—the end of a pleasantly exhausting day. In a month's time we'd do it all again.

Carolyn Hall

Carolyn Hall

Breads and Breakfast

Prairie Meals & Memories: Living the Golden Rural

Carolyn Hall

Church Ladies and Bake Sales

When you drive through the patchwork of roads in Central Kansas you see two things on the horizon, the grain elevator and the church steeple in the small town ahead. The church served as the heart and soul of the town and surrounding community and the ladies of the church, the Altar Society, fed them all.

After tending to their own chores, they cooked and served the local weddings, funerals and church picnics. These ladies, the chefs of the plains, could lay out a spread fit for a king. People piled their plates high with fried chicken, fork tender roast beef and all the trimmings. It took a second smaller plate to hold the samples of all the gelatin salads in every flavor and color. And then came the desserts, poppy seed kuchen (cook-en), rich chocolate cakes, heavenly angel foods, rosettes, and new concoctions made from spiffing up cake mixes with unusual ingredients. Betty Crocker would have been proud.

When a cause needed funds, you could count on the church ladies to answer the call with their best culinary efforts. Bake sales after Sunday church raised money and expanded waistlines.

Olmitz Kuchen (cook-en)

These little mounds of joy are sweet yeast dough filled with fruit or my favorite, poppy seed—called mohn in German. (I've never found them outside Central Kansas). The filling needs to be thicker than prepared pie fillings. If I don't make my own (make the day before), I use the Solo cake and pastry fillings (this recipe uses at least 3 cups of filling). These take practiced hands to get just right, but you'll find them worth the effort. Just before baking, top them with what Mom called zucker sai, a combination of sugar, flour, butter and a little corn syrup. Grandma added an extra touch. She drizzled the kuchen fresh from the oven with her "burned butter" (browned butter) and an extra sprinkle of sugar to make them sparkle (I omit this step). Warm or cold, these are bliss.
Makes about 4-5 dozen

Ingredients:

- ¾ cup milk
- ½ cup butter or margarine
- 1 teaspoon salt
- ½ cup sugar
- 2 packages active dry yeast
- ⅓ cup warm water
- 3 eggs, beaten, room temperature
- 5-5½ cups flour
- 2 tablespoons melted butter or margarine

zucker sai:

- 1 cup sugar
- 1 cup flour
- ½ cup cold butter or margarine
- 1 tablespoon light corn syrup

Carolyn Hall

Poppy seed filling:(makes about 1¼-1½ cups)
- 1 can Solo poppy seed cake and pastry filling
- ½ cup raisins, chopped fine
- ½ cup walnuts, chopped fine

or

- 1 cup poppy seeds, ground
- ½ cup sugar
- 3-4 tablespoons cream
- ½ cup raisins, chopped fine
- ½ cup walnuts, chopped fine

Fruit filling :(makes 1 cup filling)
- 1 can Solo cake and pastry filling any flavor, I prefer apricot

or

- 1 cup chopped apricots or other dried fruits such as prunes or cherries
- 2 tablespoons sugar if desired
- Water

Directions:
1. Heat milk, sugar, salt, and butter in saucepan until butter melts. Cool to lukewarm.
2. Dissolve yeast in warm water. Pour into large bowl. Add milk mixture and eggs. Gradually add 5 cups flour and mix. Turn out on slightly floured surface. Knead in enough flour to form medium stiff dough.

3. Place in greased pan and turn once. Cover. Let rise until doubled in bulk.

Zucker Sai:
1. Mix flour and sugar. Cut in butter with pastry blender until crumbly. Add corn syrup and toss until blended. Refrigerate until needed.

Poppy seed filling:
1. To 1 can Solo poppy seed filling, add walnuts and raisins and mix well.

Homemade poppy seed filling:
1. Grind poppy seed in blender (It will turn almost black and increase in volume. Continually stop blender and scrape seeds from underneath blades.)
2. Mix ground poppy seeds and sugar in saucepan. Add cream until dry ingredients are moistened enough to form a paste. Stir in raisins and nuts. Simmer over medium heat 5-10 minutes, until thick, stirring constantly. Cool.

Fruit filling:
1. Place dried fruit in saucepan. Add water to cover. Bring to boil. Remove from heat and let set several hours or overnight.
2. Put in food processor and blend slightly, do not puree. Return to saucepan and add sugar to taste. Over medium heat, simmer 5-10 minutes, stirring constantly. Cool.
3. Pinch off dough the size of a big walnut. Roll out to about a $\frac{1}{8}$" thick, 3"circle. (You'll know if it's too thin when you gather the first kuchen.) Place a tablespoon of filling in center (put in as much as

possible and still be able to close the top). Gather edges of dough together and pinch shut (pull up as little dough to prevent a thick bottom). Dip smooth side into melted butter, place buttered side up on greased cookie sheet. Top with a good teaspoon of zucker sai. Let rise 30-45 minutes.
4. Preheat oven to 350°. Bake 15-20 minutes. Remove when slightly browned.

Kolache or Kuchen? Kolaches are a Czech pastry. They're made from similar ingredients, but roll dough ½" thick and cut out with a round biscuit cutter. Make a small indentation in the center and fill with the same fillings. Add zucker sai as above or dust with powdered sugar after baking.

Aunt Carolyn's Carrot Cake
This birthday cake favorite features Grandma's garden fresh carrots.
Serves 16

Ingredients:
- 2 cups flour
- 2 cups sugar
- 2 teaspoons cinnamon
- 1 teaspoon baking soda
- ½ teaspoon salt
- ¾ cup oil
- 3 eggs
- 2 teaspoons vanilla
- 2 cups grated carrots
- ½ cup chopped walnuts
- 1 cup canned crushed pineapple with juice
- 1 cup raisins, boiled and drained—better yet, soak raisins in rum overnight and drain
- Frosting:
- 4 cups powdered sugar
- 2 tablespoons vanilla
- 1 4-ounce package cream cheese
- ⅓ cup butter or margarine
- ¼ cup chopped walnuts

Directions:
1. Preheat oven to 350°. Grease 3-8" round cake pans.
2. Mix dry ingredients together. Stir in oil, eggs and vanilla.
3. Add carrots, nuts, crushed pineapple and raisins. Mix well. Divide evenly into baking pans.
4. Bake 30-35 minutes or until toothpick inserted into center of cake comes out clean. Cool 10 minutes

and remove from pans. Frost when completely cool.
5. *For Frosting:*
6. Beat together cream cheese and margarine. Add vanilla. Slowly add powdered sugar, mixing well after each addition. Beat until desired spreading consistency.
7. To assemble, place one cake layer on plate and spread top with frosting, add another cake layer and frost the top, add last cake layer and frost the top. Use remaining frosting for the sides of the cake. Spread chopped nuts on final top layer.

Prairie Humor
A Kansas farmer met up with a Texas farmer at a livestock auction.
"How big of spread do you own?" asked the Texas farmer
"400 acres, more or less." The Kansas farmer replied. "How 'bout you?"
"Well sir, I can get in my pick-up and drive all day and never get to the other end."
"I had a truck like that once myself." said the Kansas farmer.

Bohemian Poppy Seed Cake

This cake calls for so much poppy seed, you'd better not have a drug screen scheduled for a few days. It has a sweet, rich flavor all its own. This is an old family favorite. The original recipe says to bake it in a slow oven until done, but I've included baking directions for those using actual temperature controls. We ground our poppy seed in an old fashioned coffee grinder. The new coffee grinders won't work. Blend 1 cup at a time in the blender. The gray seeds turn black and cake together when properly blended. The volume increases as it grinds. Whenever a recipe calls for poppy seed, I always grind it first to bring out the flavor. This recipe makes a thin batter. Use butter cream frosting from the Sunflower Cake, page 59.
Serves: 18

Ingredients:
- ¾ cup butter or margarine
- 3 eggs, whipped good
- 2 cups sugar
- 2 cups ground poppy seed
- 2 cups milk
- 2 cups flour
- 2 teaspoons vanilla
- 3 teaspoons baking powder

Directions:
1. Preheat oven to 350°.
2. Cream butter and sugar. Add eggs, one at a time, blending after each. Mix in poppy seed and vanilla.
3. Stir flour and baking powder together. Add alternately with milk, ½ cup of each at a time, starting with the flour mixture and ending with it also. Blend well after each addition.

4. Pour into 2-9" well greased baking pans. Bake 25-30 minutes. A toothpick should come out clean when placed in the center of the cake.
5. Cool 10 minutes and remove from pans. When completely cool, frost.

Poppy seed can cause false positives for opiates in urine tests, something we never had to worry about.

Prairie Info
We lived in the flatlands on the edge of the flint hills. From our farm, we could clearly see the Galatia grain elevator 11 miles away.

Prairie Fact
Hutchinson, Kansas has the world's longest grain elevator—½ mile long and holds 46 million bushels of grain.

Prairie Fact
Ellis County Kansas, location of St. Fidelis Church, the Cathedral of the Plains (one of the 8 wonders of Kansas), is home to so many historic, native stone churches. Driving tours are available.

Prairie Superstition
If a friend or neighbor brings a gift of food, it's bad luck to return their dish empty.

Batter Up

Mom loved adventure, especially in her kitchen. She collected all sorts of recipes. She clipped them from newspapers, traded with her friends and sent off for them from the gas company, electric co-op, wheat commission and television shows. Supper could be an interesting surprise with one of her new dishes or desserts.

Dad would try anything. "With five of you girls learning to cook, I've developed a cast iron stomach." He said with a grin.

Mom had spoiled him with her cooking. Her cakes for the church bake sales got reserved in advance and never made it to the display tables. I served as her apprentice. I pulled a kitchen chair over to the counter and got to help add the ingredients. When we made cakes, I sifted the flour into the batter and then poured in the milk she'd measured in her lime green Pyrex cup.

"You need to see if we forgot anything," she'd say. What a sneak.

I had trouble keeping weight on and didn't have a big appetite. In second grade, I'd lost so much weight from having the measles, the doctor threatened to put me in the hospital. Mom knew my weakness for sweets and fed me all the cookie dough and cake batter I could handle (Grandma drew the line at bread dough). She kept my ribs from showing and I learned how to tell what ingredients went into recipes by taste.

Sunflower Cake

I used a Bundt pan for this recipe and a combination of frosting and filling to salute the state flower of Kansas. Definitely a crowd pleaser.
Serves 16

Ingredients:
- 2 cups sugar
- 2 eggs
- 1 teaspoon vanilla
- 2 cups flour
- ½ cup cocoa
- ½ cup butter, margarine or shortening
- ¾ cup clabbered milk or 1½ tablespoons cider vinegar plus enough milk to make ¾ cup
- ½ teaspoon salt
- 1 heaping teaspoon baking soda
- 1 cup boiling water

Butter Cream Frosting:
- ½ cup butter or margarine
- 1 teaspoon vanilla
- 2 tablespoons milk
- 3½ cups powdered sugar—or more

Fudge filling:
- ¾ cup sugar
- 3 tablespoons cocoa
- ¼ cup milk
- 3 tablespoons butter or margarine
- ⅛ teaspoon salt
- ½ teaspoon vanilla
- 2 teaspoons light corn syrup
- ½ cup reserved butter cream frosting
- ¼ cup miniature chocolate chips or chocolate sprinkles

Directions:
1. Pour 1½ tablespoons cider vinegar into a measuring cup, add enough milk to make ¾ cup. Let sit at room temperature while assembling other ingredients.
2. Preheat oven to 325°.
3. Cream butter and sugar. Add eggs one at a time, mixing well after each. Add vanilla and mix.
4. Combine flour, cocoa, salt and soda. Into the creamed mixture, blend dry ingredients, alternately with milk, ending with the dry ingredients.
5. Add boiling water and stir until well blended. Batter will be thin.
6. Pour into greased Bundt pan. Bake 50 minutes or until toothpick comes out clean when inserted into center of cake. Cool 10 minutes and turn out onto 10"cake plate or round cardboard cake plate. (If your Bundt cake is 12", use a 12" cake plate.)
7. For a 9x13" pan—bake 25-30 minutes at 350°, cupcakes—bake 15-20 minutes at 350°, two 2" round pans—bake 25-30 minutes at 350°.

Frosting:
1. Cream butter in small mixer bowl. Gradually add 1 cup powdered sugar, beating well.
2. Mix in milk and vanilla. Slowly add remaining powdered sugar and a few drops of yellow cake coloring to make a deep yellow color.
3. Beat until frosting reaches desired spreading consistency, adding more powdered sugar if needed.
4. Beating this frosting until light and fluffy is the secret to this recipe according to Mom and hers turned out great every time.
5. Reserve ½ cup of frosting to add to filling.

Filling:
1. Add all ingredients except vanilla and reserved frosting to a small saucepan. Bring to rolling boil for 1 minute, stirring constantly. Remove from heat and cool. Add vanilla and beat until thick. Blend in reserved frosting.
2. Pour filling into center of cooled Bundt cake.
3. Frost cake with yellow icing, being careful not to mix with filling in center of cake. Can use knife to swirl petals into frosting. Sprinkle with chocolate chips or chocolate sprinkles.
4. To serve, set cake on bed of green silk leaves.

Four Hundred and Fifty Strokes but Who's Counting

Recipe directions today make it sound easy; beat until smooth, cream butter and sugar. But that all depends on how you do the beating and creaming. Our recipes in the 1950's came with two sets of instructions, one for an electric mixer and the other by hand.

Grandma didn't like the new Mix Master appliance Mom displayed proudly on her kitchen counter. She preferred the way she learned to make cakes. We'd just gotten a new recipe book in the mail and found a recipe for a Happy Day Cake that sounded good for supper.

"Your hands are younger than mine," Grandma said and held out a wooden mixing spoon. "I'll read you the instructions."

"I'll set up the mixer." I said.

"No need for all that fuss. "This is a new 'mix-easy' recipe. Saves time and energy. Just two short beating steps. Besides, we won't have to wash up the mixer when we're done."

I gave a longing look at the electric wonder and accepted the spoon while she measured in the shortening.

"Stir till softened." She instructed.

I whisked my spoon around the bowl and mashed the lard against the sides of the bowl. Next came the dry ingredients and the milk.

"Stir till flour's dampened."

This mix-easy method wasn't so bad after all, I thought. I dampened the flour and handed the bowl to her.

"Not so fast." Grandma said. "Now beat 2 minutes with a beater or 300 strokes by hand."

"I already did the 2 steps it said I needed to. Now it's time to use the mixer, right?"

"We'll count, together while you stir." She said, ignoring my suggestion.

I wanted to meet the person who called this a mix-easy recipe. My right hand went numb so I switched to my left.

"Just the eggs now and we're done." She said.

"How many strokes this time?" I asked and blew a sigh that made my bangs stand up straight.

"Says 150 more, but to be sure and take time out to rest as necessary and scrape the bowl often," she read.

I was sure glad Mom did most of the cake baking and Grandma only baked when she found a newfangled recipe to try.

Brownie Sheet Cake

Need a luscious dessert in a hurry? This chocolate cake is moist, delicious and fast. There are two secrets to this cake, cinnamon and not over baking it. Serve warm under a mound of vanilla ice cream.
Serves 48

Ingredients:
- 2 cups flour
- 2 cups sugar
- 1½ teaspoon soda
- ½ teaspoon salt
- ¼ cup cocoa
- ½ cup butter or margarine
- 1 cup water
- ½ cup salad oil
- 2 beaten eggs
- 1 teaspoon cinnamon
- 1 teaspoon vanilla
- ½ cup buttermilk or sour milk (1 tablespoon vinegar + enough milk to equal ½ cup)

Icing:
1. ½ cup butter or margarine
2. ⅓ cup milk
3. ½ cup cocoa
4. 3½ cups powdered sugar (1 pound)
5. 1 teaspoon vanilla
6. 1 teaspoon cinnamon
7. ½ cup nuts, chopped fine

Directions:
1. Preheat oven to 375°.
2. Mix flour, sugar, soda, salt and cocoa in large bowl. Set aside.
3. In small saucepan, combine butter, water, and oil. Heat to boiling stage. Stir into dry ingredients.
4. In another bowl, whisk eggs, cinnamon, vanilla and sour milk. Blend into mixture in large bowl. Stir until well blended. This is a thin batter.
5. Pour into well greased 11"x18" pan. Bake 18-20 minutes or until toothpick inserted in the center comes out clean.

Icing:
1. While brownies bake, prepare the frosting.
2. In a medium saucepan, combine butter, milk and cocoa. Bring to boil, stirring constantly. Remove from heat. Add powdered sugar, cinnamon, and vanilla. Whisk until smooth.
3. Pour warm frosting over cake as soon as removed from oven. Spread gently. Sprinkle with nuts.

Carolyn Hall

Night Life on the Farm

Farmers take things in stride. As my dad said, "What else you gonna do?"

You can't fight nature. Storms bring hail and damaging winds. Drought can stop a harvest before the wheat can even break through the top soil. And when teenagers discover the opposite sex—well that's a whole new breed of trouble.

Mom had a rule about dates. "When you get home, I'll allow 20 minutes with the yard light on before you need to come in." She'd remind my sisters before every date came to the door to pick them up—no honking for them to run outside either.

True to her word, she'd wait the 20 minutes and then blink the light. That would seem like a good system but leave it to a little brother and sister to upset the fruit basket.

We'd hear the car pull in the driveway. My sister's boyfriend, Gary, made a good target. His red Chevy Impala had a thundering muffler and he'd always announce his arrival with a few pumps on the gas pedal to shake the house windows a bit.

"Looks like Ronnie Lou's back." Mom said and noted the kitchen clock. Johnnie and I waited our chance. Once Mom left the kitchen, one of us stood lookout for her return and the other quietly opened the door to the porch and blinked the yard light.

You could here his car pipes rumble the whole quarter mile back to the highway.

Ronnie came in the house, slammed the front door and hollered, "Mom!"

"You're in early," Mom said as she came back into the kitchen.

"We weren't even home 5 minutes. Why'd you blink the yard light?"

That was our cue to disappear. But you couldn't get far in our farm house.

We paid for our sins, from Mom and the offended sister. But we were slow learners.

With the yard light off limits, we ventured into extortion. This time we waited for the light to flicker and started our attack. We'd crawl out of bed, head out the back door, sneak around the house and wait out of sight near the front porch. Just before the lip lock, we'd make our move.

"What you doing?" we'd ask.

"Why aren't you in bed?"

"We just wanted to tell you guys good night."

"That's what I'm trying to tell your sister."

"Go ahead, we don't mind."

This became a lucrative enterprise. We collected quarters or whatever treasures the guys could find in their pockets. One empty handed guy even went back to his car and gave me his wooden school ruler. I've kept it to this day.

Mom must have seen the humor in this because we carried on our toll booth unscathed for quite awhile.

Revenge doesn't always come swiftly. Gary, our main victim, who became my brother-in-law, waited patiently for my dating days. He'd become a lineman for the telephone company and installed telephone lines and poles. He brought out an old telephone pole and set it up in our yard on the farm and attached the biggest light he could find. The same kind of mammoth fixture went up on the old pole from his dating days.

"I've been waiting for this night for a long time." He said with a wink.

Mom held the door open while he switched on what seemed like 10,000 watts of daylight after my senior prom.

Prairie Wit
When I introduced my sister Rose to the first boyfriend I brought home for Sunday dinner, she asked him her prized question. "Are you the type of guy who goes out on Saturday night and sows his wild oats and then goes to church on Sunday and prays for crop failure?"

Sweetheart Roll

The way to a man's heart is through his stomach, maybe that's why Mom made these cinnamon delights for our favorite beaus on Valentine's Day.
Makes two large heart shaped loafs

Ingredients:
- ¾ cup milk
- ½ cup sugar
- 1 teaspoon salt
- ½ cup butter or margarine
- 2 packages active dry yeast
- ⅓ cup warm water
- 3 eggs, room temperature
- 5½-6½ cups flour

Filling:
- 1 cup chopped pecans
- 1 cup sugar
- 2 tablespoons cinnamon
- ¼ cup melted butter or margarine

Glaze:
- ⅓ cup evaporated milk
- 2 tablespoons brown sugar
- 1½ cup powdered sugar
- 2 teaspoons vanilla

Directions:
1. Combine milk, sugar, salt, and butter in small saucepan. Heat over low heat and stir until butter melts. Cool to lukewarm.

2. In warmed large bowl, dissolve yeast in warm water. Add cooled milk mixture and stir in eggs.
3. Gradually add 5 cups of flour and mix. Turn out on slightly floured surface. Knead in enough of the remaining flour to form a moderately stiff dough. Knead until smooth and satiny, about 5 minutes.
4. Place in a clean, greased bowl, turn once. Cover. Let rise in a warm place until doubled in size, about 1 hour.
5. Combine cinnamon, sugar and nuts.
6. Divide dough in half. Roll out one portion to a 15x10"rectangle. Brush with half the melted margarine and sprinkle with half the cinnamon, sugar and nut mixture. Roll as for jelly roll.
7. Place on greased baking sheet. Fold half the roll on top of the other half. Seal the two ends together. Starting at the folded end, cut with a scissors down the center of both halves. Fold the sides down gently and shape into a heart. Repeat with remaining dough.
8. Let rise in a warm place until nearly double, 30 to 45 minutes. In the meantime, preheat oven to 350°. Bake for 25 to 30 minutes. Do not over brown.
9. Combine evaporated milk and brown sugar in small saucepan. Cook over medium heat just to boiling stage, stirring constantly.
10. In mixing bowl, add powdered sugar, vanilla and milk mixture, beat on medium speed until creamy, about 2 minutes. Drizzle half of glaze on each heart loaf.

Son's Up, Works for Me

Farmer's are practical folks. If they can team hard work and life lessons together, it's a good day. Our neighbor's son got home a little late from his Friday night date—or should I say early? His dad decided to beat the summer heat and had headed out to plow at 5:30 a.m. He met his teen age son coming down the driveway. His dad stopped the tractor and traded vehicles with his boy.

"Since you're already up, you might as well plow." He said to his son.

Farm kids learn—usually from experience; you can have your fun, but those darn chores will be there waiting for you when you get home.

Hobbles: Metal hooks that fit over the back of a cow's hind legs. They had a chain that stretched between the cow's legs to keep them from kicking during milking. A handy device to restrain the movements of high strung young heifers.

Hobble Stone: What my brother-in-law, Gary, called the oversized high school ring I wore when I went steady with my boyfriend. Another handy device to restrain high strung young heifers.

Prairie Superstition
For a good night's sleep, make sure the head of your bed always points North.

Rise and Shine Coffee Cake

You can substitute your favorite variety of fruit pie filling in this pastry style delight.
Makes 24 squares

Ingredients:
- 2 cups flour
- 1 cup sugar
- 2 teaspoons baking powder
- ½ cup butter or margarine
- 1 egg plus enough milk to fill 1 cup
- 1 20-ounce can cherry pie filling

Topping:
- 1 cup flour
- 1 cup sugar
- ½ cup margarine

Directions
1. Cream butter, slowly beat in sugar. Combine flour and baking powder. Add to first mixture alternately with milk and egg, mixing well after each addition.
2. Preheat oven to 350°. Grease 10½" x 15" jelly roll pan. Spread batter into pan.
3. Spoon cherries from pie filling randomly over batter. Drizzle remaining pie filling between cherries.

For the topping:
4. Mix flour, sugar and cut in margarine to a coarse grain. Spread mixture evenly over batter. Bake 30-35 minutes.

Carolyn Hall

Prairie Know-How

Mom used a piece of straw from our broom to test for doneness of her cakes. One busy afternoon, she entrusted me to check on the cake. Luckily, she caught me before I pierced her prize recipe.

"Always break the straw from the top near the handle, not from the bottom we've been sweeping the floor with all week." She said and sent me back for a clean straw.

Clabbered milk: Our fresh cow's milk wasn't pasteurized. Mom would measure out the amount for her recipe and let it sit on her windowsill at least a day. It soured naturally and became very thick and curdy. I usually forgot to clabber the milk ahead of time so she taught me a shortcut with vinegar—add 2 tablespoons of vinegar and add enough milk to make 1 cup.

Prairie Tip
A new straw broom will last longer if it's soaked in strong salt water before using.

Prairie Wisdom
Don't count your eggs for baking, measure them instead. Each egg should equal ¼ cup of liquid. Eggs come in different sizes and don't all yield ¼ cup. For example, 3 eggs should equal ¾ cup. If not, add water or more of the liquid called for in the recipe to yield ¾ cup. This will keep your baked goods moist and consistent.

Prairie Meals & Memories: Living the Golden Rural

Carolyn Hall

Reunited For the Holidays

The magic of Christmas at our house happened around 2 a.m. on Christmas morning. That's when we shared the best of the season.

Santa had already made his rounds—we always got an early delivery, just before dinner on December 24th. Only a few stray bows and remnants of wrapping paper remained under the tree when Mom would announce. "Anyone going to Midnight Mass needs to be ready by 10:30." With a house full at Christmas, the best she could hope for was 11:00. "We won't get a seat if we don't get there early."

Some of the family tried to get in a catnap but the excitement in the air kept the sandman at bay. Beside the toys, everyone got something new to wear and you had to be seen in it at Mass. If I asked nicely, Grandma would iron my new plaid dress for church—Dad picked one out every year.

We sang Christmas Carols all the way home from church and Mom wiped the condensation off the inside of the windshield with her gloves so Dad could find the road.

"Get those good clothes off and I'll set the table." Mom said when we got back in the house.

We dashed to get in our pajamas and head back to the kitchen. The aroma of fresh brewed coffee greeted us. Mom had her own secret for instant coffee. She'd fire up the burner under the aluminum tea kettle that resided over the pilot light on the gas stove. It gave us a source of constant warm water and a head start for coffee. In no time, the kettle whistled and steamed. She poured it directly over a pile of ground coffee in a saucepan, then strained it through a thin screened strainer. Hot chocolate with marshmallows filled mugs for the younger generation.

"Grace first." Grandma insisted when my brother reached for his cup. We bowed our heads and prayed in unison.

Mom whittled the remains from the Christmas country ham, filled a platter and passed it around the table. Home made bread followed and we feasted on sandwiches and reruns of the delicious holiday dinner.

"This is my favorite time of the year." Dad said. Mom's eyes echoed his words.

We talked and laughed—shared memories and dreams. Dad would carry the sleepyheads to bed and share precious alone time with Mom. I rarely think of my parents and not see them setting together in the yellow glow of the kitchen light on that holiday at 2 in the morning.

We lost Mom nearly twenty years ago and Dad joined her not long ago. I know they're together sharing those memories. You see, he left us on Christmas morning at the magic hour.

Prairie Meals & Memories: Living the Golden Rural

Carolyn Hall

He Knows if You've Been Bad or Good

On the evening of December 6 each year, my brothers, sisters and I could hardly contain ourselves waiting for the knock on the door. It was St. Nicholas Day, and the German tradition meant he would secretly leave brown paper bags bulging with fruit, nuts and candy on our doorstep. That's assuming we were on good behavior the previous year-- otherwise we could expect a big thorny stick. A loud knock on the door signaled his delivery. We held our breath, and looked at each other for reassurance before opening the door, not sure what we'd find.

Our St. Nick, as we called him, had a soft heart, no sticks in sight. We gathered around the kitchen table to sample our loot, while Dad shared his childhood memories of St Nicholas Day in Odin, Kansas, where he grew up.

"St. Nick came in person, but not alone." Dad said. His eyes narrowed as he described the sidekick. "A boy dressed all in black, carrying a gunny sack over his shoulder came along. He brought it to take the bad children away with him."

We squirmed as Dad described the sack.

"You could see legs hanging out of the side of the bag." He shook his head and lamented, "It wasn't a pretty sight."

"I'm glad we were good," I said, not wanting to meet the fate of those terrible children.

I never dreamed I'd someday move to Germany and celebrate St. Nick in his land of origin with my own children. We discovered our teenage neighbor, Thomas and his friends, earned their Christmas money by bringing St. Nicholas to life in our village of Buch. We arranged to meet with Thomas, who spoke fluent English and hired him for the job.

"Leave whatever presents you have for the children on your doorstep. We'll arrive around 7 this evening," he said.

Just after supper, the sound of bell ringers drew us to the window. Down the street came Thomas dressed as St. Nicholas. He wore the crimson and white robes of a Catholic bishop, with a flowing white beard and a tall pointed hat. He carried a six-foot staff that barely reached his head. Boys carrying lighted candles surrounded him. Just behind him in the shadows skulked someone dressed all in black. On one shoulder he carried an overstuffed burlap bag and a bundle of long, gnarled sticks on the other. And yes, extremities dangled from his sinister sack.

The wide-eyed look of disbelief on my children's faces was priceless. They'd heard many tall tales from their grandpa, and thought St. Nicholas traveling with this disreputable character was just one of them. Now, they watched him in the flesh walk up their front steps. They huddled together, remembering their past year's transgressions.

"We've been mostly good, haven't we Mom?" Dawn, my five-year-old daughter asked.

"We'll see what St. Nick thinks about that," I said as the doorbell rang.

We opened the door and invited Thomas and his band of boys inside. My kids dove behind me, their heads peeking out cautiously at our guests.

"Wait quietly for me in the next room." Thomas instructed. "I have something to discuss with your mother."

No need to ask them twice. They disappeared in a flash.

"What are your children's names?" He whispered as he opened a large gold foil covered book. "Tell me something good each of them has done recently and also something you want them to improve on." He took notes in his book as I spoke.

He motioned for his group to follow, turned and headed into the living room. Dawn and Clay sat wide-eyed holding each other's hand. Thomas called them to him one at a time.

"Dawn," he said and opened his book and ran a thin finger down the page half way and stopped. "I see you help your mother with your baby sister, Lisa. I'm very proud of that." He retrieved a bag of goodies from one of his assistants, handed it to her and patted her gently on the head. Then he returned to his book traced a page on the opposite side, shook his head and frowned. He motioned the dark character forward and took a long thin stick from him. Dawn shot me a concerned look. Thomas handed it to her. She timidly accepted the stick that towered several feet above her.

"Dawn, I see that you fight too much with your little brother. I want this stick to remind you to do better." She nodded her head and remained perfectly still as she stood on her tiptoes at full attention.

Next my three year old Clay took his turn. Thomas repeated the same routine, recounting the good and bad deeds recorded in his book. Both children stood motionless, a stick in one hand and a sack of goodies in the other.

Thomas looked at them and said, "Remember what I've told you and help your baby sister learn the same. I'll be watching, and I'll be back next year to see how you're doing." With that, the group left as solemnly as they arrived.

The bells trailed off in the distance as St. Nicholas continued his rounds.

We returned to Kansas City the following year. St. Nick came that next December, but with just a knock at the door, like I'd had as a child.

"St. Nick has too far to travel to meet with everyone," I explained. "But next week you can see Santa Claus."

We went to the local mall and waited our turn to see the man in red. Dawn sat on his lap and visited with him, but I couldn't hear the conversation. She came running back, holding a small bag of goodies.

"Did you have a nice talk with Santa?" I asked.

"Sort of, but he sure doesn't know very much. He had to ask *me* if I'd been good."

Chocolate Cashew Clusters

Everybody's favorite at Christmas. Add variety with different nuts. Dry roasted cashews, dry roasted peanuts, or red skinned peanuts. At the end of the batch, with more chocolate left than nuts, I add a few raisins for an additional treat. We used to make these on top a double boiler on the stove, but the microwave saves time and dishes. These freeze well.
Makes about 3-4 dozen

Ingredients:
- 2 cups semi-sweet chocolate chips (1-12 ounce bag)
- 12 ounces almond bark, broken into small pieces
- 2½-3 cups dry roasted whole cashews

Directions:
1. Put chocolate chips and almond bark in microwave safe bowl. Microwave 2 minutes on high. Remove and stir. Return for another 2 minutes. Remove and stir vigorously. Return for an additional minute of cook time if lumps remain. Microwave ovens vary, you may need to adjust for difference. Do not over cook.
2. Add nuts and stir until coated. Drop by teaspoonfuls onto waxed paper.

Impossible Toffee Cracker Candy

A surprising chocolate toffee confection made with saltine crackers. Fast, easy and so delicious you may want to give it as gifts.

Makes 3 dozen 'pieces'

Ingredients:
- 40 saltine crackers. (1 sleeve)
- 1 cup butter or margarine
- 1 cup brown sugar
- 2 cups semi-sweet chocolate chips (12-ounce bag)
- 1 cup chopped pecans or walnuts

Directions:
1. Preheat oven to 400°.
2. Line a greased jelly roll pan (10½" x 15½") with saltines.
3. Combine sugar and butter. Bring to boil over medium heat, stirring constantly. Boil for 4 minutes. Pour mixture over saltines. Spread to cover.
4. Bake 5 minutes. Remove from oven and scatter chocolate chips on top. Return to oven for 1-2 minutes or until chocolate begins to melt. Remove from oven. Spread chocolate evenly over pan. Sprinkle with nuts. Refrigerate until hardened. Break into pieces to serve.

Vanilla Moons

A delicate hand formed butter cookie that's been our Christmas tradition passed down through generations. The original recipe says to bake in a slow oven until just done. For those who like specifics, the baking time and temperature are suggested below. This recipe doesn't require leavening with baking soda or baking powder. The almonds need to be ground to bring out the oil that helps hold the cookies together. Put away your mixing spoon, the warmth of your hands helps make this dough come together.
Makes 6-7 dozen

Ingredients:
- 1 cup sugar
- 3 cups flour
- 1½ cups almonds, blanched and ground fine
- 1½ cups butter or margarine

Vanilla sugar coating:
- 1½ tablespoon vanilla
- 2 cups powdered sugar

Directions:
1. Combine all ingredients into a large bowl.
2. Work dough with your hands to mix.
3. Shape dough into 2 long rolls, 2" in diameter. Cover with waxed paper and freeze several hours or overnight.
4. Preheat oven to 300°. Turn off.
5. Pour powdered sugar in shallow baking pan, sprinkle with vanilla. Place in oven until dry. (I leave overnight.)

6. Put dried sugar mixture in blender and process until fine and free of lumps. Return to baking dish.
7. Preheat oven to 325°.
8. Slice cookie dough in ¼" slices. Cut in half and form each into a crescent moon shape. Place on cookie sheet. These can be placed closer together than most cookies as they do not rise.
9. Bake 10-15 minutes until set. Do not brown. Ovens vary so check often.
10. Remove from oven and let set 1-2 minutes. Using long spatula, lift off cookies and place in vanilla sugar. Sprinkle sugar generously over cookies to coat. Do not allow cookies to cool before coating as it sticks to warm cookies best.
11. Move cookies to paper towels to cool. They freeze well.

Our gas oven had a broken knob with no visible numbers for temperatures. We set the temperature by the height of the gas flame on the burners below the oven. A ¼ inch flame meant a slow oven, a ½" high flame a moderate setting and an inch high flame caused Mom to ask if you meant to burn the house down. I wondered why Mom never bothered to get a new knob until I remembered she used to cook with a wood burning stove and oven and she knew when the oven "felt" right. Her 'flame height' method just helped the inexperienced bakers in the family feel more secure.

I Remember Mama's

Mom searched for years for the perfect version of a German Christmas Stollen recipe. Much like Santa Claus, the Easter Bunny and the Holy Grail, tales of this infamous sweet bread abounded, but she couldn't find it.

"My mama made Christmas braid every year," Dad reminisced. "She made it so big, we kept pieces clear up to Easter. It had to be at least this tall." He said and held his hand a foot above the kitchen table. Sure wish you'd have learned to make it before she died."

Mom sighed and rested her chin in her hand. She'd never remembered seeing or tasting it during the few Christmases she knew her mother-in-law.

Mom came from an Austrian-German family, Dad's from north-central Germany. Just a small change in geography can make a big difference in traditional foods and customs then and now. She scoured recipe books, wrote her sisters-in-law and checked magazines trying to find the recipe Dad remembered.

Finally, one Christmas during my holiday break from college, she announced, "I think this is it." Mom said. "Your dad always said it had white frosting decorated with candied cherries and almonds. That's what this recipe calls for."

We hurried and baked the new rendition. It had all the elements, candied fruit, almonds, and two braids of dough stacked on top each other and baked.

"Lay those braids down gently on top of each other. I want this to rise as big as possible." She instructed.

Christmas Eve supper would be the great unveiling. Mom kept it out of sight until the last second. She proudly sliced the first piece and handed the plate to Dad.

We all watched his face. Mom held her breath.

"Good. But I think Mama's was taller." He said and measured another few inches above her braid. "Maybe more fruit and nuts too."

Mom sounded like a balloon that lost its air. She chuckled, shook her head and served the rest of her creation. We cleared the table after supper and started the dishes.

"If I doubled the recipe, it still wouldn't be right." She said and smiled. "You shouldn't compete with a special memory. It'll always be better."

I moved to Germany and lived there nearly 2 years. Dad retired and my parents came to visit Germany for the first time. They both spoke fluent 'Platte Duetsch' (Americanized Low German) and felt a real kinship with the people and country. I lived 60 miles and a mountain range from my dad's father's birthplace. We visited Dad's first cousins a number of times, once just before my parents left in late December.

As usual, our cousin Helen prepared a bountiful brunch. This time, she added a lovely petite loaf of bread, covered in powdered sugar with raisins and candied fruit peaking through the crust. Mom and I traded grins and our cousin noticed.

"Stollen, sehr gut." she said.

Mom nodded in acknowledgement and said, "Yes, very good."

Christmas Stollen

You can find many variations of this bread and God knows Mom tried her share. This one became Mom's favorite, which she called 'Vanocka'. A trick I learned in Germany is to soak the fruit and almonds in brandy, rum or Kirsch (cherry liqueur) overnight. Some Germans keep the last pieces for Easter—Dad was right about that. Commercially made Stollen have marzipan or almond paste centers. This makes a pretty Christmas brunch bread.

Makes 2 Loaves

Ingredients:
- 2 packages yeast
- ¼ cup warm water
- 2 cups scalded milk
- ½ cup sugar
- ½ cup butter
- 1 egg beaten
- 2½ teaspoons salt
- ½ teaspoon almond extract
- ½ cup rum
- 1 cup blanched almonds
- 1 cup golden or dark raisins (or half of each)
- 1 cup mixed candied fruit
- 5½ cups flour
- 4 tablespoons melted butter

Carolyn Hall

Glaze and decorations:
- 2 cups powdered sugar
- 3 tablespoons milk
- 1 teaspoon vanilla
- ½ cup candied red and green cherries (can use pieces of candied fruit leftover from the bread)
- ½ cup blanched almonds

Directions:
1. Place 1 cup raisins and 1 cup candied fruit in rum, stir to coat. Soak overnight. Drain the fruit before using in recipe, reserve the liquid.
2. Dissolve yeast in warm water. Cream sugar and butter. Add egg, salt, almond extract and reserved rum. Stir in cooled milk and yeast. Add 2 cups flour. Beat until smooth. Let rise ½ hour.
3. Toss fruit and 1 cup almonds with 2 tablespoons flour. Add to the above batter and mix well.
4. Add remaining flour ½ cup at a time to make a soft dough. Knead until smooth and elastic on floured board, incorporating more flour as needed. Dough will be soft, add extra flour sparingly.
5. Place in greased bowl and turn once. Cover and let rise until doubled in bulk.
6. Cut dough in half. Set one aside. Divide first half into 5 elongated strips. Braid 3 strips and place on greased cookie sheet. Twist the remaining 2 strips and place on top of the braid. Pinch the ends together.
7. Brush loaf with 2 tablespoons of melted butter.
8. Repeat for second part of dough.
9. Let rise covered, 1 hour or until doubled in bulk.

10. Preheat oven to 350°. Stagger loaves in oven for better heat circulation. Bake 45 minutes. Transfer to wire racks to cool.

Glaze and decorations:
1. Combine milk, sugar and vanilla. Mix until smooth.
2. Pour glaze over slightly warm braids. Spread with knife for complete coverage.
3. Decorate the braids with the candied fruit and almonds.

Apricot Filled Cookies

These cookies taste like pastries—not surprising because they call for yeast. Use Solo Apricot Filling for best results. It's thicker than pie filling. Jelly and jam have no thickener and will cook out during baking. These cookies freeze well, but layer them with waxed paper to prevent sticking together.
Makes about 4 dozen

Ingredients:
- 1 can Apricot Solo Cake & Pastry Filling 12-ounce can
- 3 cups flour
- 1 tablespoon sugar
- ½ teaspoon salt
- 1 cup butter or margarine
- ½ cup milk
- 1 package active dry yeast
- 1 egg, slightly beaten
- ½ teaspoon vanilla
- powdered sugar

Topping:
½ cup powdered sugar

Directions:
1. Combine flour, sugar and salt. Cut in margarine.
2. Scald milk. Cool to lukewarm and add yeast. Add egg and vanilla, mix.
3. Add flour mixture and blend by hand. Divide dough into 4 parts.
4. Roll each part to about ⅛" thickness on surface dusted with powdered sugar. Cut out circles with a biscuit cutter (about 2½" diameter).

5. Place teaspoon of filling in each center. Take two edges and pinch shut at top. Fold sealed edge down on top of cookie.
6. Place on greased cookie sheet, 2" apart. Let rise 10 minutes before baking.
7. Preheat oven to 350°. Bake 10-12 minutes. Do not brown.
8. Remove from cookie sheet and sprinkle with powdered sugar.

Bakery Bread And Margarine

Our family raised, butchered or made almost everything we ate. Eating out meant going to the church picnic or a wedding dinner, full of homemade delights, except when we made a trip to Hays, sixty miles away, for their big summer sales day. On the way home we'd stop at the grocery store for groceries and lunch fixins. Mom drove and my sisters and I would deal out the bread and lunchmeat in the backseat and make sandwiches. A 'community' carton of juice got passed around to wash them down, followed by sugar wafers; chocolate, strawberry and vanilla.

"This is the best." I said and snagged another slice of bread. "Sure wish we could have bakery bread all the time. It's so soft."

"Grandma makes good bread too." Mom reminded me.

I loved her homemade bread, hot from the oven, but when it got cold, the crust turned tough. I wished we had bakery bread everyday but Monday, her bread-baking day.

Grandma made butter too, from the cream we separated from the milk, at least until Mom got sick. She suffered two strokes before I turned twelve. Things got scary for a while. She had to learn to walk and talk again, twice.

"I have to watch what I eat, the doctor says." Mom told me. "No more butter or egg yolks. I need to drink skim milk and no more bacon or lard either. I should lose a little weight too"

Grandma put away the jar we saved the grease in after frying bacon. She had used it to fry her famous hash browns and wilt her lettuce. A bottle of corn oil stood in its place on the stove. Mom converted all her cake and cookie recipes too. The ingredient list read butter or margarine but she used the latter every time.

"Good thing we have lots of eggs," mom said while she cracked and separated the whites into a bowl. "I can make all the angel food cakes I want because they're made with egg whites and no fat."

Mom loved chocolate and it didn't take long for her to concoct a chocolate angel food cake recipe that became a community favorite.

Mom refused to let her diet restrictions get the best of her. She cut her ice cream splurges back to one trip a month to Dairy Queen. She invented her own homemade margarine from corn oil and powdered milk, but she had her rebel moments.

"Where did you get that new mixing bowl?" I asked.

"It's not a mixing bowl, it's my new Tupperware measuring cup." She said, showing me the gradations marked on the side. "See, here's the receipt. It says I bought a 2- quart measuring *cup*."

I watched her fill it to the brim with freshly popped popcorn. Dad bought her an air popper that required no fat or oil. He knew she loved her popcorn almost as much as she loved ice cream.

"How much popcorn are you supposed to eat at a time?" I asked.

"The doctor said I can have one cup a day." She said tossing a kernel in her mouth. "He just didn't say what size cup."

Strength of will, KU Medical Center and prayer, kept mom with us until the age of 72.

Mom's Chocolate Angel Food Cake

This light and delicious cake really melts in your mouth. Mom's egg whites came straight from the hens. She sifted and resifted her dry ingredients four times into a chocolate-laced mountain of sugar and flour on waxed paper, no lumps allowed. Use a wide-mouthed large bowl if possible to fold in the dry ingredients to give more surface area to incorporate the dry mixture. Chocolate butter cream frosting finishes the confection perfectly, see page 90. This makes a big cake. It will rise 1"-2" above the cake pan. Use the egg yolks to make homemade noodles, recipe page 115.
Serves 14-18 large slices

Ingredients:
- 6 tablespoons cocoa
- 1 cup + 5 tablespoons sugar
- 1 cup + 2 tablespoons flour
- 2¼ cups egg whites, room temperature (about 16)
- 2¼ teaspoons cream of tartar
- 2¼ teaspoons vanilla
- 1 cup + 2 tablespoons sugar
- ½ teaspoon salt

Directions:
1. Preheat oven to 375°.
2. Sift cocoa, flour, and 1cup + 5 tablespoons of sugar four times. Set aside.
3. Measure egg whites, cream of tartar, vanilla and salt into LARGE grease free bowl. Beat until foamy. Gradually add the 1 cup + 2 tablespoons of sugar, 2 tablespoons at a time, while beating egg white mixture until stiff peaks form but not dry.
4. Gently fold in the flour mixture with a spatula, 2 tablespoons at a time. Continue until dry ingredients disappear in batter. Do Not Stir.
5. Push batter carefully into ungreased 10" tube pan (angel food cake pan). Use a table knife to cut gently through batter several times in circular motion to remove air pockets and combine any white streaks in chocolate.
6. Bake on lowest rack for 45-55 minutes or until done. Do not open the oven door for the first 30 minutes or cake may fall. Cake develops deep cracks in the top as it bakes. Remove from oven when cake springs back if touched lightly.
7. Invert immediately over bottle to hang until cooled, at least 1 hour. Loosen cake from pan and remove. Frost if desired with Chocolate Cream Frosting.

Prairie Wisdom
Don't slam the kitchen door while mom's angel food cake bakes in the oven. A jolt like that could cause her cake to fall and send you to exile with your nose stuck in a corner.

Chocolate Cream Frosting

This makes a chocolate angel food cake doubly chocolaty delicious. For a mocha treat, substitute the milk for ¼ cup strong coffee.

Ingredients:
- 6 tablespoons butter or margarine
- 4¼ cups powdered sugar
- ½ cup cocoa
- 1½ teaspoons vanilla
- ¼ cup milk
- 2 tablespoons boiling water

Directions:
Cream butter. Add the cocoa and half the powdered sugar. Beat well. Add vanilla and milk, continue beating. Gradually add remaining powdered sugar while mixing. Add boiling water and whip until soft and creamy. Add more boiling water if needed for spreading consistency, a teaspoon at a time.

Prairie Tip
Buy a two-piece angel food cake pan with a removable center. The stem in the middle should be wide enough to fit over a long neck bottle; beer or wine work well.

Carolyn Hall

Cattle Crossing

For most kids, Old McDonald's Farm taught them their animals and the sounds they made, to me it recited the critters on our farm. We had the pigs, chickens, ducks, geese and of course, cows—milk cows to be exact.

We kept milk cows as opposed to stock cattle which are raised primarily for meat. Our "Bossies" earned distinctive names and some even a place in our heart. Dad believed in variety, so our herd contained several dairy breeds and the resulting cross breeds. The Brown Swiss, mild mannered but stubborn, the Jerseys with their cream rich milk but over protective of their newborns, (Buttercup gave me a boost over the wooden gate with her head when I got too close to her baby calf), the Guernseys, docile and colorful with their red and white splotched hide and the Holsteins, the black and white standard issue dairy cow. The cows are tame but watch out for the bulls, they can turn vicious.

I ran the nursery on the farm. Once weaned from their mothers, I bottle fed the calves until they were old enough to join the herd in the pasture. Playing with the calves became my pastime. They followed me like ducklings and we would race around their pen, occasionally they would butt their heads at me, especially the bull calves. I never got hurt and thought their playful nods rather cute.

One of my little guys grew into a 2000 pound bull. A robust Holstein, Dad decided to keep him as the bull for the herd. No longer a calf, his antics became intimidating. True to his nature, he'd rake dirt into the air, bellow and on occasion, charge. My brother got chased in the pasture and I jumped onto the side of the truck when the bull didn't like me getting out to pitch silage in the corral. We all went on alert around the bull. When he wasn't kept in a different pasture, Dad usually took on the task of herding the cattle.

On a foggy morning in early spring, Dad started to move the cattle to the wheat pasture across the highway. He got them headed out and then hurried to get to the road to watch for cars. The bull took Dad down from behind and butted him into the ground. Our dogs, one a German Shepherd, bit at the bull's heels to scare him away, but the bull continued his assault. Fortunately, a neighbor driving by saw the attack and drove his car into the field, honking to no avail. He got out and used a tire iron to hit the bull. The distraction worked long enough to get Dad into the car before the bull turned his attack on the car, crushing a fender. Dad went to the hospital with serious shoulder injuries and the bull got rounded up and taken to the meat packing plant.

Dad needed major surgery to have nearly every nerve and tendon repaired in his shoulder. In early summer, he went to the University of Kansas Medical Center in Kansas City, Kansas, nearly 250 miles away, to have the operation. He returned in a plaster cast that covered most of his upper body and propped his injured arm in the air even with his ear.

"This may seem extreme," the doctor said, "but we need it to heal in this position so you can eventually raise your arm to this height."

It was late June and harvest time. Farming doesn't come with sick days. Your paycheck depends on you beating the weather and getting your crops to market. The rest of us could handle the day to day chores, but Dad was the combine driver. He climbed aboard our International Harvester machine and headed to the amber waves with difficulty. He made the first round on the eighty acres, the same field he had been herding the cattle toward the day he got hurt, when he stopped and looked toward the highway. A line of combines and wheat trucks crested the horizon and converged on our farm. Our friends and neighbors cut the crop in nearly a day and returned in a few weeks with an army of tractors to turn the wheat stubble under as well.

People talk about a Midwest Ethic. It goes beyond hard work and determination and it's a humbling sight to see first hand.

As for Dad's shoulder, he didn't settle for raising his arm to his ear. I watched him throw a towel over the bathroom door several times a day and pull his injured shoulder up with his good arm. His grimace told us his pain but he never stopped.

"If I baby it, I'll have a baby arm." He'd say, regaining his smile.

To his doctor's amazement, he regained nearly 100% use of his shoulder and over the next few years, helped do repairs on most of those combines that came to his rescue that harvest day.

Prairie Oysters

Rocky Mountain oysters, cowboy caviar, calf fries, this dish has many names. But the plain fact is they're fried bull testicles. Freeze before preparing for easier skinning and slicing. Dip in your favorite spicy sauce. Makes about 2 dozen

Ingredients:
- 2 pounds bovine testicles, (calf are smaller but more tender)
- 2 cups beer
- 2 eggs, beaten
- 1½ cups flour
- ¼ cup yellow cornmeal
- salt and fresh ground pepper to taste
- oil for frying

Directions:
1. Heat oil in deep fryer to 375°.
2. Remove skin and cut each into ¼"-½" slices.
3. Place in large bowl and cover with beer. Marinate 2 hours.
4. In another bowl, mix eggs, flour, cornmeal, salt and pepper.
5. Remove testicles from beer, drain excess liquid. Dredge in flour mixture.
6. Deep fry 3 minutes or until golden brown. Pieces rise to the top when done.
7. Serve with beer, preferably Coors Light from a keg.

Prairie Folklore
Eating prairie oysters will make a man out of you, no matter what it did to the previous owner.

Best Ever Meatloaf

A staple served up on every farmer's table along with mashed potatoes, green beans and chunky applesauce. Cooks well in the microwave 12-15 minutes on high. For a change of flavors, substitute barbecue, picante or chili sauce for the ketchup. Save any leftovers for meatloaf sandwiches the next day.
Serves 4-6

Ingredients:
- 1 pound lean hamburger
- 1 medium onion, chopped
- 1 cup chopped celery
- 2 tablespoons cooking oil or margarine
- 1 egg, beaten
- ½ cup ketchup
- ¾ cup oatmeal
- ¼ cup milk
- salt and pepper to taste

Directions:
1. Preheat oven to 350°.
2. Sautee onions and celery in oil until soft.
3. Mix hamburger, salt, pepper, oatmeal, ketchup, milk and egg. Stir in onions and celery and blend well. Let set 15 minutes at room temperature to soften oatmeal.
4. Shape into loaf and place on rack set in baking pan. Bake 50 Minutes. Let stand 10 minutes before cutting.
5. Microwave alternative: Put in greased microwave safe dish, a bundt style works best, or form meatloaf in a ring with 2" center. Microwave on high for 12-15 minutes. Let stand 10 minutes before cutting.

Sloppy Joes with Beans

When we had a bumper crop of tomatoes, we'd can our own tomato soup and use it to make this hearty hot sandwich. Commercial tomato soup makes a good substitute with a lot less fuss. Serve over a toasted bun with sassy pickles and a fresh spinach salad.

Serves: 4-6

Ingredients:
- 1 pound hamburger
- 1 large onion, chopped
- ½ cup brown sugar
- 2 cans condensed tomato soup (10¾ ounce size)
- 1 tablespoon mustard
- ¼ cup ketchup
- 1 can pork and beans (15 ounce size)
- ½ teaspoon chili powder
- salt and pepper to taste
- 4-6 hamburger buns
- butter or margarine
- 1 cup shredded cheddar cheese

Directions:
1. Brown hamburger and onions in large skillet. Drain grease.
2. Add brown sugar, soup, mustard, ketchup, pork and beans, and spices.
3. Simmer 20 minutes, stirring occasionally.
4. Butter hamburger buns. Broil until golden brown.
5. Spoon hamburger mixture over buns. Top with shredded cheddar cheese.

Oven Barbecued Beef Brisket
Serves 6-8

Soak overnight:
6 lbs brisket

Marinade:
- 4 ounces liquid smoke
- 1 tablespoon celery salt
- 1 tablespoon onion powder
- 1 tablespoon garlic powder
- 2 tablespoons Worcestershire sauce
- 1 teaspoon ground pepper

Barbecue Sauce:
- 18 ounces commercial barbecue sauce (I use KC Masterpiece Original)
- 2 tablespoons liquid smoke
- 2 tablespoons brown sugar

Directions:
1. Mix marinade in large baking pan. Add brisket and turn one time to coat with marinade leaving fat side up. Cover tightly with foil. Refrigerate overnight.
2. Bake at 275° for 5 hours.
3. Drain juice. Stir barbecue sauce ingredients together and cover brisket with 1½ cup of sauce. Return to the oven and bake uncovered for one additional hour.
4. Heat remaining sauce and serve with sliced brisket.

Prairie Tip
Never cool down your barbecue meats with cold barbeque sauce, always serve the sauce hot, like gravy.

Prairie Fun
Try a barbecue sauce showdown at your next gathering. Serve several different brands, or recipes for sauces and have a taste testing. Have your guests vote for the crowd favorite.

Prairie Meals & Memories: Living the Golden Rural

Carolyn Hall

Starches

Prairie Meals & Memories: Living the Golden Rural

Carolyn Hall

Feed Sack Fashions

With eleven mouths to feed at our table, we went through a lot of flour. Grandma bought it by the 50 pound sack. When she got it home, she'd undo the chain-stitched top, roll the string into a ball and save it to wrap packages for the mail. Then she emptied the flour into the storage container and took the sack outside and shook out the fine white dust. It could go in the laundry now and be ready to become someone's sewing project.

Back then, flour, seed and grain companies competed for your business by selling their product in decorative cotton printed sacks we called feed sacks. Mom kept her feed sack material in a drawer in her dresser. We'd shop her stash when we wanted to sew. If we didn't have enough of our favorite print, we'd take it grocery shopping with us and try to find more of the same or a good match of another color. Our local grocery store even started selling flour, printed for pillowcases, with a decorative border along the top of the bag. A 50 pound sack fit a regular pillow perfectly, no sewing needed. I remember the day I wanted to find a mate to a pillowcase for my hope chest—I was eight, but a girl could never start planning for her future home too soon.

When Mom and Grandma headed to town the next week to do the monthly grocery shopping, I made sure I went along.

"It's my turn to pick out the flour." I reminded them and headed straight for the bakery section. They had only one of my pillowcases left. I had to act fast. An unsuspecting stocker had just finished a display of cake mixes when I asked for assistance.

"Sir, could you help me get a sack of flour up front to the check out?"

"Sure can."

He walked over to a 5 foot stack of the flour sacks and grabbed the top one, heaved it on his shoulder and turned around.

"I'll have this up front when you're folks are ready. What's the name?"

I looked up at him and shook my head. "That's not the one my Grandma wants."

"Sewing something special, huh?" He swung the sack from his shoulder and sat it on the pallet next to the stack. "Bet you need this pretty blue one right here." He said and pointed to the next one down.

"This one." I said and pointed to my pillowcase at the bottom of the pile.

101

I clasped my hands behind my back and smiled sweetly.

"Tell your folks I'll have it up there in a little while."

I gave him Grandma's name and thanked him.

Our family ate our way through bread, noodles, dumplings, and wonderful cakes and cookies, all the while providing material for everything from aprons to quilts.

Mom and Grandma usually paid for their groceries by cashing an egg money check but if it didn't cover the bill, they used a counter check from our bank. All the grocery stores, gas stations and dry goods stores kept a supply of checks from the surrounding towns' banks at their checkout counters. Back then you didn't need to remember your account number to write a counter check. You just needed to remember to log it into your checkbook when you got home.

Grandma's White Bread—Almost

Grandma's bread came from her heart and her head. She never used a recipe. This basic white bread has a healthy addition, whole wheat white flour. I've mistakenly used all-purpose flour for the recipe and it turned out good, but I prefer the added boost of the bread flour. Be sure and try the two variations, or try a flavor of your own.

Makes 2 loaves

Ingredients:
- ½ cup milk
- 3 tablespoons sugar
- 2 teaspoons salt
- 3 tablespoons butter or margarine
- 2 packages active dry yeast
- 1½ cups warm water
- 2 cups whole wheat white flour
- 3-4 cups bread flour
- Melted butter or margarine

Filling for Variation 1
½ cup sugar
2 teaspoons cinnamon
2 tablespoons melted butter or margarine

Filling for Variation 2
½ cup grated parmesan cheese
2 teaspoons garlic granules or powder
2 teaspoons dried basil
2 tablespoons melted butter, margarine or olive oil

Directions:
1. In small saucepan, add milk, sugar, salt and butter. Heat until butter melts. Let cool to lukewarm.
2. In large bowl, dissolve yeast in warm water. Add milk mixture and all the whole wheat flour. Beat

with mixer 3 minutes until smooth. Stir in 2½ to 3 cups bread flour until dough pulls cleanly away from sides of bowl.
3. Knead 10 minutes or until smooth and elastic on lightly floured board, adding flour as needed. Place in greased bowl and turn once. Cover and let rise in warm place, free from drafts 1 hour or until doubled in bulk.
4. Punch down and divide in half.
5. On lightly floured surface, roll each half into a 9"x14" rectangle. Start with short end and roll dough tightly. Pinch seam to seal. Pinch each end and turn under. (dip fingers in water before pinching dough to help seal) Place in greased bread pan with seam side down.
6. Cover and let rise 1 hour or until doubled in bulk as before.
7. Preheat oven to 400°.
8. Bake for 30 minutes. Remove from loaf pans immediately and brush tops with butter.

Variation 1
1. After rolling dough out on floured surface, spread each rectangle with half of the melted butter. Mix cinnamon and sugar and sprinkle half of the mixture onto the buttered dough. Roll and shape each loaf as before and let rise 1 hour and bake as directed above.

Variation 2
1. Roll out dough, spread with butter or olive oil. Mix cheese and spices and sprinkle on dough. Roll and shape each loaf as before and let rise 1 hour and bake as directed above.

Cake Mix Cinnamon Rolls

Dress up Sunday brunch with these homemade delights. Try different flavors of cake mixes to add your own touch to the rolls. Spice, butter pecan, caramel, or lemon all work well with this recipe. This dough may be refrigerated for 24 hours before baking after cutting and placing the rolls on the topping. Let rise until doubled in bulk before putting in the oven.
Makes 2 dozen

Ingredients:
- 2½ cups warm water
- 1 regular size caramel cake mix
- 2 packages active dry yeast
- 4½-5 cups flour

Filling:
- ½ cup butter or margarine, melted
- 3 tablespoons brown sugar, firmly packed
- 5 teaspoons cinnamon

Topping:
- ½ cup butter or margarine, melted
- 1 cup brown sugar
- 1 cup white sugar
- ½ cup light corn syrup
- 1 cup chopped pecans

Directions:
1. In small bowl, dissolve yeast in warm water.
2. Add cake mix and 3 cups flour in large bowl. Pour in yeast mixture. Stir to blend.
3. Add remaining flour ½ cup at a time. Mix well after each addition. When dough pulls away from side of bowl, place on lightly floured board and knead until smooth and elastic, about 5 minutes.

Dough will be soft. Place in greased bowl, turn once. Cover. Let rise 1 hour or until doubled.
4. Divide dough in half. Roll each into large rectangle ½" thick on lightly floured board.

Filling:
5. Mix brown sugar and cinnamon. Spread half the butter on each rectangle. Sprinkle half the sugar mixture on each rectangle. Start with long end of rectangle and roll up dough. Seal edges. Cut in ½" slices.

Topping:
6. Combine butter, sugars, corn syrup and nuts in small sauce pan and heat until sugars dissolve. Pour half of mixture into each of 2 well greased 9"x13" baking pans. Place sliced rolls on top. Cover and let rise 1 hour or until doubled.
7. Preheat oven to 350°. Bake 15-20 minutes.
8. Remove from oven and invert onto serving platter. Serve warm.

Cake mixes came into popular use in the 1950's. Homemakers used them for a base for cakes, desserts and pastries. The mixes were meant to be time savers, but the practiced cook couldn't resist putting her own creative ideas and flavors into them.

Sweet Tooth Cornbread

This variation tastes more like a quick bread and works well as muffins.
Makes 24 servings

Ingredients:
- 2½ cups cornmeal
- 2 teaspoons soda
- 1 cup brown sugar
- ½ cup butter or margarine
- 3 eggs
- 1½ cup buttermilk
- ½ teaspoon baking powder
- 1 cup flour
- 1 teaspoon vanilla

Directions:
1. Preheat oven to 350°.
2. Blend cornmeal, flour, salt, baking powder and baking soda.
3. Cream butter and sugar, add eggs and vanilla. Beat well.
4. Alternately add dry ingredients with buttermilk to creamed mixture.
5. Pour into greased 9"x13" pan. Bake 45-55 minutes until a toothpick inserted in the center comes out clean.

Sauerkraut Rye Bread

A light rye bread flavored with caraway. The sauerkraut keeps it moist and delicious. Great with smoked sausage or save leftover slices to make croutons, recipe page 127. They're a delightful surprise in soups and salads.
Makes 2 loaves

Ingredients:

- ¼ cup honey
- ¼ cup light molasses
- 1 teaspoon salt
- 2 tablespoons butter or margarine
- 2 tablespoons caraway seeds
- 1 cup chopped sauerkraut, drain and reserve liquid
- Enough water added to reserved sauerkraut liquid to make 1 cup
- 2 tablespoons mustard
- 2 packages active dry yeast
- ¾ cup warm water
- 2 cups rye flour
- 2 tablespoons cocoa powder
- 1 cup whole wheat white flour
- 2½-3 cups bread flour

Directions:

1. Bring water mixed with reserved sauerkraut liquid to boil. Place honey, molasses, salt, butter, mustard, caraway seeds, and boiling water mixture in small bowl. Stir until all dissolved. Cool to lukewarm.
2. Dissolve yeast in ¾ cup warm water in large bowl. Add the cooled boiling water mixture, rye flour,

cocoa, sauerkraut, and 1 cup whole wheat flour. Mix with electric beater until well blended, about 1 minute, scraping sides of bowl as necessary.
3. Work in bread flour to form a stiff dough, adding flour ½ cup at a time. Turn out on floured board and knead 8-10 minutes or until dough becomes soft and elastic adding remaining flour as necessary.
4. Place dough in greased bowl, turning once to grease top. Cover. Let rise in warm place about 1 hour or until double in size.
5. Punch down and divide in half. Shape each into a round loaf. Place on two greased cookie sheets. Cover. Let rise in warm place about 1 hour or until doubled in size.
6. Preheat oven to 350°. Bake 40-45 minutes. Remove from cookie sheets and cool on wire racks.

Sunflower Oatmeal Bread

Great for sandwiches or toasted with butter and jam, this whole wheat bread is surprisingly light with a satisfying crunch.
Makes 2 loaves

Ingredients:
- 1 cup warm water
- 2 packages active dry yeast
- 1 cup milk
- ¼ cup butter or margarine
- ⅓ cup honey
- 1 egg
- ½ cup sunflower seeds
- 2 teaspoons salt
- 1 cup oatmeal
- 2 cups white whole wheat flour
- 3½-4 cups all-purpose flour

Topping:
- 1 egg white, beaten
- 1 tablespoon water
- 1 tablespoon oatmeal

Directions:
1. Scald milk. Stir in butter and honey. In large bowl, dissolve yeast in warm water. Blend in salt, egg and cooled milk mixture. Add oatmeal, 2 cups of whole wheat flour and 1 cup flour. Beat until smooth with electric mixer about 1 minute. Stir in sunflower seeds.

2. Work in remaining flour, ½ cup at a time. Add enough flour to make dough handle easily. Turn out on floured board. Knead for 8-10 minutes, adding flour so dough is not sticky.
3. Place in greased bowl, turn once. Cover. Let rise in warm place, free from drafts for 1 hour or until doubled in bulk.
4. Punch down dough and divide in half. Shape each into loaf and place in greased bread pans. Cover. Let rise in warm place, free from drafts for 1 hour or until doubled in bulk.
5. Preheat oven to 375°. Beat egg white and water together with fork. Brush tops of loaves with mixture. Sprinkle with oatmeal.
6. Bake 35 minutes. Remove from pans. Immediately cool on wire racks.

Old Fashioned Pie Crust

Mom taught me to make this on the old Formica kitchen tabletop. I've since converted to using a bowl, the large yellow Pyrex one she handed down to me. We always made it with homemade lard, pure and snow white—rendered carefully for baking. For those watching their diet, they ate the filling and left the crust. Nowadays, I use butter or margarine. If you don't want to put the egg in your crust, brush the bottom crust with a slightly beaten egg white if you're making fruit pie. It prevents the juice from soaking into it and the crust will bake nice and crisp. The vinegar makes the crust extra tender, so don't forget it. Be sure all your ingredients are well chilled. In warmer weather, you may want to refrigerate it for at least 30 minutes after mixing to make it easier to handle. Add the ice water a tablespoon at a time, you want to use as little as possible—just barely enough to make ingredients stick together. This is a rich pastry and a little hard to handle, but well worth it. For left over pie dough, see the recipe on page 114 for Cinnamon Crisps.
Makes about 3 large pie crusts

Ingredients:

- 3 cups flour
- ½ teaspoon salt
- 1 teaspoon vinegar
- 1 egg, slightly beaten

- 1 cup lard, shortening, butter, or margarine (butter or margarine needs to be well chilled)
- 3 tablespoons ice water (Mom kept an ice cube or two in it while we mixed the dough)

Carolyn Hall

Directions:
1. Mix flour and salt in large bowl. Cut in lard and work until pieces are no larger than a pea.
2. Beat egg, vinegar and 1 tablespoon of ice water together. Stir into flour mixture with a fork. Sprinkle ice water, one tablespoon at a time as needed. Blend sparingly, until ingredients are moistened. Best if chilled 30 minutes before using.
3. Roll out on surface lightly dusted with flour to ⅛" thickness, and 2" greater in diameter than pie pan.

Cinnamon Crisps

Let the kids practice rolling pie dough with this recipe. Don't roll out more than once or twice—it'll get too tough. This makes a fun snack while you wait for the pie to bake. Make as much cinnamon sugar as needed for amount of dough left.

Makes as much as you have left over

Ingredients:
- Leftover unbaked pie dough
- 1 tablespoon soft butter or margarine
- ¼ teaspoon cinnamon
- 1 tablespoon sugar

Directions:
1. Preheat oven to 450°
2. Mix cinnamon and sugar.
3. Roll dough to ⅛" thickness. Spread lightly with butter. Sprinkle with cinnamon mixture as desired. Cut into 1"x 4" strips or desired shapes. You can also leave it whole and break apart after baking.
4. Bake 10 minutes or until brown.

Grandma emptied her 50 pound sack of flour into a large metal can with a tight fitting lid. She kept it in an unheated storeroom off the porch. Every Sunday night in winter, Dad carried the can into the kitchen and set it next to the furnace. Monday was Grandma's bread baking day and it wouldn't do to have cold flour.

Egg Yolk Noodles

This is a good way to use leftover egg yolks from making angel food cakes. Grandma always kept us on the edge of our seats when she made noodles. She'd hang a tea towel over the back of the kitchen chairs, and drape her rolled out noodle dough over them to dry. We dared not lean back in our chairs at lunch. Use these in soup or make Noodles in Burnt Butter recipe on page 116.
Makes 4 batches

Ingredients:
- 3 cups flour
- 6 egg yolks
- 1 teaspoon salt
- 6 tablespoons water (about)

Directions:
1. Stir salt into flour. Beat egg yolks and water. Put flour mixture on a clean surface and make a well in center. Pour egg yolks and water into center. Mix with hands until dough becomes stiff as possible, but workable. Add a *little* more water if necessary. Knead until it forms a ball.
2. Divide into 4 balls. Roll very thin. Drape tea towels over chairs and hang noodles on them to dry separately. When almost dry and do not stick together, prepare them to cut.
3. Roll dry dough jellyroll fashion (can stack more than one sheet together to roll). Cut into desired widths. Lay on baking sheets in dry place. Cover with cloth and let noodles dry thoroughly, turning once. Bag and freeze if desired.
4. To serve, boil in large pot of salted water or chicken broth until done, about 20 minutes.

Noodles in Burnt Butter

Grandma heated butter in the skillet until it turned brown. She called this her burnt butter, though she never let it get that far. It brings a full-bodied taste to the butter and makes any dish taste rich and mellow. She'd use her homemade Egg Noodles recipe on page 115, but you can use store bought and I won't tell. Don't wander off while making any part of this recipe, it needs constant attention. You can also add very small fresh bread cubes to the burnt butter and sauté briefly before pouring over the noodles.
Serves 4-6

Ingredients:
- ¼ homemade noodle recipe or a 12-ounce package of store bought noodles
- salt to taste
- water for cooking
- ¼-½ cup butter (depends on how rich you want them)
- 1 teaspoon cinnamon
- ¼ cup sugar

Directions:
1. Cook noodles in lightly salted water for 20 minutes or until tender. Drain. Return to pot.
2. Heat butter in heavy skillet over medium high heat. Let brown. Stir constantly—do not let it burn. Pour over noodles. Sprinkle with cinnamon and sugar and toss. Serve immediately.

Prairie Wisdom
Give a farmer flour, eggs, butter and milk and his family will never go hungry.

Carolyn Hall

Soups, Stews and Casseroles

Prairie Meals & Memories: Living the Golden Rural

Carolyn Hall

No Kissing Cousins, Please

When small farms filled the Kansas landscape in the 1950's, it took large families to keep up with all the work. My Dad's family set the standard for large. He had thirteen sisters and three brothers that survived to adulthood. On the way to family reunions, which had to be held at the big city park in Great Bend, we'd see who could name all the aunts and uncles the fastest.

All Dad's brothers and sisters married and the family grew exponentially from there.

I married, had my kids and moved many times. Keeping in touch with my own parents and siblings took priority and I lost contact with most of my cousins.

In the 1980's I returned to Kansas City and this time took root. My daughter Lisa came home from junior high and announced she had a new student teacher and they both had a Grandpa named John Boor. I knew this couldn't be any niece of mine, so I called my Dad. Turns out, she was his great-niece—I'm not good at deciphering cousins once removed, but she was family all right.

I figured the time had come for "the talk". I gathered my three kids and told them the dating pool in Central Kansas would be filled with relatives.

"Don't date anyone west of Topeka without checking with your Grandpa first."

. . . . . .

When my Grandpa Boor died in 1955, at age 86, his obituary listed 17 children, 91 grandchildren, and 34 great-grandchildren. Of those 142, 129 survivors lived in Kansas. At the time, it was believed to be a record for the state.

Old Fashioned Ham Bone Soup

You can't wait to finish the ham so you can use the bone for this delicious soup. Be sure and sort the beans and check for rejects and pebbles. Yes, there can be small rocks in the package. The one time I didn't check, I found one just before I added the ham. Serve with Sweet Tooth Cornbread, recipe on page 107.
Serves 8 to 10

Ingredients:

- 1 pound dry navy beans, (about 2 cups)
- 2 quarts water
- 1 meaty ham bone or 2 cups ham pieces
- 1 cup carrots, sliced thin
- 1 cup celery, sliced thin
- 5 whole peppercorns
- 1 large onion chopped
- 1 bay leaf

Directions:

1. Rinse beans. In Dutch oven, add beans and 2 quarts of water. Bring to rapid boil, reduce heat and simmer 2 minutes. Remove from heat, cover and let stand 1 hour.
2. Add remaining ingredients. Simmer 1½ to 2 hours, stirring frequently until beans are tender.
3. Recipe can be made in slow cooker. Pre-cook beans as above. Add all ingredients and cook on low for 10 to 12 hours or on high for 5 to 6 hours.

Creamy Corn Chowder

Nothing takes a bite out of a Kansas winter like a steaming bowl of soup. Add a side of Fancy Apples (recipe on page 21) with slices of warm garlic and cheese beer bread and you'll be ready for those chores in the morning. After adding milk mixture to soup, do not bring to a boil, it could curdle the milk.
Serves 6 to 8

Ingredients:
- 2 heaping cups potatoes, diced
- 1 cup carrots, thinly sliced
- 1 cup celery, thinly sliced
- 1 large onion, chopped
- 1 tablespoon chicken base, or 3 bouillon cubes
- pepper, to taste
- ⅓ cup butter or margarine
- ⅓ cup flour
- 2 cups milk
- 1 cup + ¼ cup grated Parmesan cheese
- 1 can cream style corn

Directions:
1. Add 3 cups water, potatoes, carrots, celery, onion, chicken base, and pepper to large saucepan. Bring to a boil. Simmer covered over medium heat until vegetables are fork tender, about 10 minutes.
2. While vegetables are cooking, melt butter or margarine in medium saucepan. Stir in flour until well blended. Gradually add milk, stirring constantly over medium heat until thickened and bubbles break on the surface. Add 1 cup cheese and cook 1 to 2 more minutes until cheese is blended.

3. Pour cheese mixture into cooked vegetables. Add creamed corn. Stir occasionally over medium heat for 5 to 10 minutes. Do not let soup come to a boil.
4. Garnish with additional Parmesan cheese.

Cooking Tip
To avoid spills and splashes when pouring liquid from one pot into another, pour it slowly over the back of a wooden spoon held in the other pot.

Al & Theresa's Green Bean and Dumpling Soup

I learned to make this recipe in their kitchen. Al has been perfecting his dumplings for most of his 80+ years. He shared his top secrets, make them small and don't over mix the dumpling dough or they'll get tough. Serve with fresh fruit, a cheese plate and homemade bologna (recipe page 159)
Serves: 8

Ingredients:
- 1 large onion, diced
- 1 large potato, peeled and diced
- 4 stalks celery, diced
- 2 16-ounce cans green beans
- water
- salt and pepper to taste
- 1 quart cream (fat free cream works fine)
- 1 tablespoon dried parsley flakes
- ¼ cup minced garlic

Dumplings:
- 4 eggs
- ½ cup milk, or cream
- 1 teaspoon salt
- 2½-2¾ cups flour

Directions:
1. Spray large, heavy saucepan with non-stick cooking spray. Add potatoes, celery and onion. Cook over medium heat, stirring constantly until vegetables start to soften and brown. Add ½-¾ cup water if necessary to prevent sticking.

2. When softened, add enough water to double the depth of the vegetables. Stir in green beans and minced garlic.

Dumplings:
1. While soup simmers, beat eggs. Add ½ cup milk, salt, 2½ cups flour. Stir until blended. Do not over mix. Add more flour if needed to make a thick, sticky dough.
2. Drop by teaspoon into soup. When dumplings float to the top, remove from heat.
3. Stir in salt, pepper, parsley and cream.

Prairie Exterminator
Don't try this at home. Gardeners picked the beetles off their potato plants and dropped them in a bucket of kerosene.

Rueben Soup

All the favorite flavors in a comfort food version. Serve with rye bread croutons (page 127) and a winter fruit salad recipe (page 17).
Serves 6-8

Ingredients:
- 1 medium onion, chopped (1 cup)
- ½ cup celery, chopped
- 3 tablespoons butter or margarine
- ¼ cup flour
- 3 cups water
- 4 teaspoons beef base or 4 beef bouillon cubes, crushed
- 8 ounces corned beef, shredded
- 1 cup sauerkraut, drained
- 3 cups light cream (fat free cream works fine)
- 1½ cup shredded Swiss cheese

Topping:
- rye croutons (see below)
- 1 cup shredded Swiss cheese

Directions:
1. In large saucepan, cook onion, celery and beef base in butter until vegetables are soft. Stir in flour

until smooth. Add water gradually and bring to boil. Reduce heat and simmer 5 minutes, stirring occasionally.
2. Add corned beef, sauerkraut, cream and cheese. Cook and stir 30 minutes.
3. Serve topped with rye bread croutons and grated Swiss cheese.

Rye Bread Croutons
Makes 3 cups

Ingredients:
- 6 slices rye bread
- 2 tablespoons butter or margarine, melted
- salt and pepper to taste

Directions:
1. Preheat oven to 375°.
2. Trim crusts from bread. Cut into ½" cubes.
3. Stir salt and pepper into butter. In large bowl, toss bread cubes with butter mixture.
4. Put bread cubes on greased baking sheet. Bake 5-10 minutes until crisp and starting to brown, stirring occasionally.

Prairie Meals & Memories: Living the Golden Rural

Did You Hear the One about the Farmer's Daughter Who Went To Boston?

When I walked the pastures as a little girl, I thought the horizon ended at the next farm. My view of the world changed when I attended college.

"You can be anything you want to be," Mom said, "you just have to apply yourself."

Farmers were farmers from birth to death. What would I want to do for the rest of my life?

I tried on a few different majors and finally settled on becoming a dietitian. I'd watched Mom change her diet after her strokes and surgery for her clogged arteries. As for knowing about food, I had first hand experience from the ground up. It seemed like a good fit.

Before I could change majors though, I'd have to change schools. KU didn't offer a dietetics degree so it meant a transfer to K-State. Going from a Jayhawk to a Wildcat would be like changing sides in a battle, a traitor to the colors. I needed to be sure about this decision.

"You'd better be sure you like working in a hospital," Mom advised.

"Good idea." I said and applied to several hospitals for a summer job—all in Boston. My high school sweetheart went to school there and would be staying for the summer. Seemed like a win-win situation to me. Besides, I'd survived going from a high school with 116 kids to KU with over 19,000 students. How much harder could it be working in Boston? City life with subways and skyscrapers sounded like an adventure I'd like to try.

Mom didn't let me see her worry lines when I told her, but she kept her rosary close. Now, all I had to do was find a job working in a hospital dietary department.

"You need a resume to send out," my sister Rose said when I called her.

"Write down anything you've ever done," she said. "You never know what might catch their eye and decide to give you an interview."

I perused my sparse list of experience; farm work and babysitting professors' kids. "Are you sure someone in Boston wants to know I can milk a cow and drive a tractor?" I asked.

"Put it down, it can't hurt."

Eighteen and intrepid, I sent my job request to several Boston hospitals. To my surprise, I got three interviews. Two involved a lot of dishwashing, but the third responder agreed to talk to me about being a diet aide, working directly with patients. I saved my babysitting money and flew up during spring break to make the rounds of the hospitals that sent me a positive response.

After two offers that would give me dishpan hands, I didn't hold out much hope when I stepped in the door of Massachusetts General Hospital. With at least nine different hospitals attached to one another and seven different kitchen facilities, it was its own city.

I found my way to the main dietary department and double-checked the office number on the letter I'd been sent. It was my golden ticket.

I stopped at the secretary's desk and showed her my sweat stained paper with the hospital's logo on top, signed by Mae Dozier, Head of Dietary Personnel.

"Miss Dozier's expecting you." She said and led the way to a small office across the hall.

"Come in and sit down," Miss Dozier said. "I hope I haven't wasted your time."

A vision of thousands of dirty plates and cups flashed through my mind. I took a deep breath and braced my ninety-nine pounds for the news.

"I really shouldn't be interviewing you for this position," she said. "We usually look for more experience for our summer relief help, but I've never met anyone who's driven a tractor and plowed a wheat field. I had to see you for myself."

She peered at me over her glasses balanced on the end of her nose and began reading.

"As a diet aide, you'd be in charge of passing out and retrieving menus, supervising patient tray prep to ensure the proper diet, discussing food preferences, and delivering snacks." She arched one eyebrow at me to solicit a response.

"I grew up in a family on special diets," I explained. "I can cook, and I help with the meal planning at my house at school. I studied a lot of nutrition during four years of high school home economics…"

She raised her hand and smiled. "If a tiny thing like you can maneuver a tractor through a field in Kansas, I think you can do the job for me. We'll start you off in pediatrics. It's a smaller unit to break you in. You'll start May 26."

"Mom, I got the job." I screamed after she accepted the charges for my collect call from Boston.

"I had no doubt."

"You okay with it?"

"You've got a good head on your shoulders; I know you'll use it. Besides, I didn't hold your hand at KU, Boston's just a little farther.

Mom would have liked my boss if they'd met. Miss Dozier had a special nickname for me. It wasn't unusual for me to hear the page, 'Caroline from Kansas'. She wanted to say Dorothy but thought that went a bit too far.

Ranch Style Baked Beans

This is a meatier version of Boston Baked Beans and takes a lot less time to cook.
Serves 8-10

Ingredients:
- 1 pound lean hamburger
- 1 envelope onion soup mix
- 2 cans pork and beans (15-16 ounce size)
- 1 can kidney beans, drained
- 2 tablespoons brown sugar
- 2 tablespoons molasses
- 1 cup barbecue sauce
- ½ cup water
- 2 tablespoons prepared mustard
- 2 teaspoons vinegar
- ¼ cup green pepper, chopped, optional

Directions:
1. Preheat oven to 350°.
2. Brown hamburger in large skillet or saucepan, drain grease. Stir in remaining ingredients.
3. Pour into large casserole and bake 45 minutes until hot and bubbly.

Prairie Tip
Who needs gum? Just put a small handful of wheat in your mouth and chew.

In Kansas, a 'house divided' means you've got one kid at KU and the other at K-State.

Prairie Pastime
We'd lie on a mound of grain in the back of the wheat truck and make wheat angels. They're a lot warmer than snow angels and our backsides stayed dry.

The Jayhawk is a mythical bird whose history dates back to the 1850's and the fierce battles to keep Kansas a 'Free State' in the slavery issue.

Rock Chalk Jayhawk, part of the KU chant, came from chalk rock, another name for limestone, found on the KU campus and throughout Kansas.

Carolyn Hall

Hoof, Feather and Fin

Carolyn Hall

The Cows Are Out

"Get up." Mom said shaking my shoulder. "The sheriff called, the cows are out on the county blacktop."

She kept a flashlight at her bedside for just such occasions, no need to wake the whole house by turning on all the lights. (Grandma and Uncle Frank were exempt from late night cattle drives.) The beam from her Eveready flashlight highlighted the radio alarm clock, 3 a.m... We'd need to be up for 7 o'clock mass in a little over two hours.

"Dad's got the car running, let's go." We pulled our clothes on over our pajamas, grabbed extra flashlights and headed for the car.

"Did you get some pliers and wire in case we have to fix the fence?" Dad shouted from the idling Chevy.

"Got it." Mom answered.

You never knew what you'd find once you got there. Snipe hunters or a late night Casanova parking and sparking with his girlfriend may have left the gate open, or a heifer might have broken through the fence trying to get to the clover just out of reach in the ditch. No matter, you had to corral them before a neighbor boy out past curfew broadsided a bovine, or the cows could make it to the wheat field.

If they got in the green wheat this late in the season, it not only would taint the flavor of the milk, it would stunt the wheat harvest. Dad grew wheat as a dual-purpose crop. He'd graze the cattle until it grew to the first joint in the stem. The cows couldn't be on it any longer after that or it wouldn't make a head for the grain come harvest in late June.

"Lucky there's a full moon," Dad said.

We found the escapees in the ditch next to the fence, only five had made a break for it. Someone had left the three-strand barbed wire gate lay on the ground instead of hooking it back up. Once we got the runaways surrounded, we herded them back toward the opening. They always played dumb, as if they'd never gone through that gate before.

"I'm gonna be full of chiggers tomorrow," I complained.

"At least we don't have to stay out walking the fence line looking for a hole," Mom said.

Dad painted an old tire with "No Trespassing" and hung it around the fence post at the gate the next day. "Hate to be unneighborly," he said. "But I hate chasing cows in the middle of the night a lot more."

Sauerfleisch

Mom's version of sauerbraten, either way it sounds better in German. It translates sour meat or roast. Don't let the name fool you. It's rich and delicious. We originally made this recipe using home canned meat we'd put up in jars and pressure-cooked. There's nothing tastier. We'd reheat it with the ingredients below. No need to roast it, it came out of the jars fork tender. You can substitute low fat sour cream with good results. Mom made this with or without gingersnaps depending on supplies on hand. Serve over mashed potatoes. Serves 10

Ingredients:
- 4 pounds round steak, cut in 1" cubes
- water
- 2 onions, sliced thin
- 4 carrots, sliced
- 3 cloves garlic, minced
- ¼ cup fresh celery leaves
- 2 bay leaves
- 2 tablespoons mixed pickling spices (make sure there are several whole cloves in this)
- 10 peppercorns
- salt to taste
- ½ cup sour cream
- ½ cup gingersnaps, crushed or ¼ cup flour
- cheesecloth or clean white cotton rag
- cotton string

Directions:
1. Cut 5" square of cloth. Fill center with peppercorns and mixed pickling spices. Gather ends together to make sack and tie shut tightly with cotton string or ½" strip of cotton cloth.

2. Place round steak in roaster. Cover with water, vegetables, salt, bay leaves and bag of spices. Cover and marinate in refrigerator at least 2 days.
3. Preheat oven to 350°.
4. Bake 2½ hours in covered roaster in the marinade. Remove from oven. Strain meat juice into large saucepan. Keep vegetables warm. Mix sour cream and gingersnaps or flour. Stir into meat juice and cook until gravy is smooth and thickened. Do not allow to boil.
5. Add meat to gravy, stirring to coat. Serve vegetables on the side.

Prairie Wisdom
Rub the end of the lip on cream pitchers with a bit of butter or salad oil to keep them from dripping.

Steak Fingers

A touch of onion and garlic liven up these steak delights. Take out your frustrations pounding this meat into tender strips, you'll love the result. You can substitute boneless chicken breasts for the round steak. Serve with honey mustard sauce (recipe on page 139).
Serves 4-6

Ingredients:
- ¼ cup butter or margarine
- 2 eggs, beaten
- 2 teaspoons water
- ⅔ cup fine breadcrumbs
- ¼ cup grated parmesan cheese
- salt and pepper to taste
- ½ teaspoon garlic powder
- ½ teaspoon onion powder
- 2 pounds round steak, tenderized
- ¼ cup flour

Directions:
1. Heat oven to 400°. Add butter to 9"x13" baking dish. Set in oven to melt.
2. Cut steak into 1" strips.
3. Mix eggs and water, beat till blended. Mix breadcrumbs, cheese and seasonings.
4. Dredge steak strips in flour, dip in egg mixture and then roll in breadcrumbs. Place in baking dish. Bake uncovered, 20-25 minutes. Turn and continue baking 15-20 minutes longer until golden brown.

Honey Mustard Sauce
Substitute spicy hot mustard for a stronger version. This tastes great as a salad dressing too.
Makes 1½ cups

Ingredients:
- ½ cup honey
- ¾ cup ginger ale
- 1 tablespoon cornstarch
- ¼ cup prepared mustard
- ½ teaspoon prepared horseradish

Directions:
1. Combine all ingredients in small saucepan.
2. Cook and stir over medium heat till sauce is thickened and glossy. Do not boil.

Bierocks

A German meat-filled roll stuffed with ground beef, cabbage, onions and sauerkraut. Different cooks add their own secret ingredients, such as ground pork, sausage, garlic powder, vinegar and even cheese. You can use different breads for the dough. I've used a hot roll mix, crescent rolls, frozen roll dough, and made from scratch bread dough. How much time I have determines whether I make the bread dough from scratch. Make the filling the day before and refrigerate—it's easier to handle. This recipe makes enough to freeze. They reheat well for a quick snack or a meal.
Makes 18-20

Ingredients:

Filling:
- 1½ pounds hamburger
- 1 medium head cabbage, shredded (about 6 cups)
- 1 large onion, chopped
- salt and pepper to taste
- 1 can sauerkraut (15 ounce can), drained
- ¼ cup melted butter or margarine

Roll Dough:
- 1 cup milk
- ½ cup sugar
- 1 tablespoon salt
- ½ cup butter or margarine
- 2 packages active dry yeast
- 1 cup warm water
- 6 cups flour
- 1 egg, beaten
- ¼ cup butter or margarine, melted

Directions:
1. Brown meat until pink disappears. Drain. Add onion and cabbage and simmer covered about 15 minutes, or until tender. Stir in sauerkraut. Salt and pepper to taste. Cool.

Dough:
2. Scald milk, add sugar, salt and ½ cup margarine. Cool.
3. In large bowl, dissolve yeast in warm water. Stir in milk mixture and egg. Add 3 cups flour and beat until smooth.
4. Work in additional flour until dough pulls away from edge of bowl. Turn onto floured surface and knead until smooth and elastic adding more flour if needed, 6-8 minutes.
5. Place in greased bowl, turn once. Cover and let rise till doubled in size 1-1½ hours.
6. Punch down and roll out in long strips. Cut into 4-5" squares. Pack a ⅓-½ measuring cup with filling, I like a lot of filling. Pull sides of dough up to the center and pinch shut. Place on greased cookie sheet, smooth side up. Brush with melted butter. Cover and let rise 30 minutes.
7. Preheat oven to 350°. Bake 30 minutes or until golden brown. Serve warm.

Frozen Roll Dough Alternate
Thaw overnight in refrigerator. Work 2 rolls together, roll out, fill and close. Brush with butter. Place on cookie sheet. Cover and let rise 30 minutes. Bake as above.

Prairie Meals & Memories: Living the Golden Rural

Carolyn Hall

Meat, Poultry and Fish

Prairie Meals & Memories: Living the Golden Rural

It Takes A lot of Guts To Make Sausage

Butchering time meant a new batch of Dad's homemade German sausages (wurst). Family recipes and know-how traveled to this country in the 1800's and passed to the next generations. The black cast iron sausage press had been a fixture for as long as I could remember. I'd fight for my turn at the crank and watch the meat mixtures snake into long ropes of sausages. It was a delight to see the table top disappear under the lengths of stuffed casings.

"Slow down, you're getting air pockets." Dad warned. He'd have to cut the casings if they weren't tight enough, squeeze the meat and plump up the sausage and tie off the end.

"I learned this trick from my dad when I was your age." He said.

Liverwurst, blood sausage and Dad's famous smoked sausage served as staples at our table and for many of our neighbors too. Sausage making was a community event. Our kitchen table hosted the crew. Dad ground the meat and added his spices to taste.

"All meat. No fillers." Dad said and dug into the washtub full of meat with both hands up to his elbows. He mixed 40 pounds at a time and tested for just the right flavor in each batch. I helped with the tasting too, even the blood sausage until I got old enough I wrinkled my nose when Dad poured in the fresh blood.

"Put your finger in and take a bite. See if it's got enough flavor. You're not afraid of a little blood?" Dad asked.

Dad never turned down an eating adventure, especially during butchering. When my sister-in-law Judy helped for the first time, he pulled his usual trick. He boiled hogs' heads on the kitchen stove to make his renowned 'head cheese'—a special sausage he made, and then stuffed it in the cleaned out stomach of the animal to cure. At lunch time, he'd slice off one of the cooked pig's ears, and put it between to slices of bread. Always the generous host, he always offered it to the newcomer first.

"Good eating. Try it." After getting the typical shudder response, he'd down his delicacy in three bites.

Dad always shared his creations and my kids developed a taste for Grandpa's sausage.

We lived in Kansas City and tried to time some of our homecomings to Dad's wurst making adventures.

Sharing my childhood traditions with my kids made the event memorable. We crowded around the old kitchen table, Dad's same friends came to help and he of course pulled the famous pig's ear trick on each of the kids.

The dimly lit room erupted with the savory smells of time-tested recipes. No exhaust fan here, the yellow-painted plaster walls sweated greased rivulets of moisture—Dad was making head cheese again. The kids washed out the pans and copper kettles they nearly had to crawl inside to clean. I opened the purchased casings and soaked them in salt water to thaw. Dad mounted the sausage press on the table and Mom measured and cut the white cotton string we'd tie each sausage with. Grandpa's practiced hands taught each child to thread the yards of casing onto the stuffing tube at the bottom of the press. They delighted as I did to watch the casings balloon to life as they turned the crank. They learned to 'eyeball' the meal size portion of each wurst and used the cotton thread to tie off each end and snip it free from the longer length still attached to the tube. Occasionally we'd have to rescue a small finger tied to the end of a sausage by an errant knotting maneuver. We made all the family favorites, ending with the smoked sausage.

For lunch, Dad fried up the various leftover sausage meat in patties. It tasted as good as it smelled.

Later the men would carry the tubs filled with the smoked sausage down to our hand-dug smoke cellar at the end of the yard. These wurst got tied in rings so they could be hung on rods in the cellar and smoked with hickory for up to 16 hours.

For meals, we boiled them in water for 10 minutes and ate them casings and all. That is until I took my kids on a trip to a local history museum in Kansas City.

Our tour guide knew all sorts of wonderful tidbits and fun facts. We toured the old brick home, completely furnished in the style of Kansas in the 1800's. The kids were amazed at the old divan with real horse-hair cushions and rope tied bed springs of the era. But when we headed to the kitchen, they told the man he'd got it all wrong.

"These aren't antiques, our Grandpa uses these all the time." Dawn, my oldest protested.

"Mom uses some of this stuff too, and I know how to use that." Clay said and pointed to a sausage press sitting next to the hearth.

"You've made sausage?" the guide said trying to retake the lead.

All three kids nodded in agreement.

"I put the stuff on that tube right there." Lisa said, squatting down to show the man. "And Dawn turned the handle and made the sausage get this big." She showed him an inflated view of the resulting wurst.

I feared what was to come and I stood at a loss to stop it. The guide kept his gaze on the kids and refused to acknowledge my waves of protest.

"Bet you don't know where that 'stuff' comes from that you put on the tube?" He asked through a toothy smile.

From the furrowed foreheads and the bitten lips, I knew they couldn't remember the word.

"Casings." I shouted hoping to end the discussion.

"Intestines. They're the intestines of the animal. Isn't that a great way to use every bit of the animal. No waste." He said.

I wanted to waste him. The damage was done and could not be repaired.

A collective "Euww" came up from the trio.

Despite my reassurances that the casings had been thoroughly cleaned and that they were then cooked before we ate them, their sausage making days were behind them. They still loved Grandpa's sausage, but they inspected every piece to be sure I'd removed the offending casings before I put them on the table.

Flatlanders used hand-dug cellars to cure their meats and save their families when a storm began to rotate and the cyclone headed for the homestead.

Big John's Smoked Sausage

Dad, known as Big John, made this sausage for over 65 years. The recipe and methods have been passed down through generations. He mixed forty pounds at a time until he had 400 pounds ready to stuff into casings. He carried it to the smoke cellar and kept the hickory fire burning all night long to cure the sausage. You can use all hamburger if you prefer. You'll need a sausage stuffer, a smoke cellar, hickory or fruitwood and a good alarm clock to wake you up every few hours to tend the fire.
Makes 40 pounds of sausage

Ingredients:
- 20 pounds fresh ground pork
- 20 pounds fresh ground hamburger
- 2 cups Lawry's seasoning salt
- 15 cups water
- 10 toes (cloves) garlic, optional
- 2½ ounce tin of coarse ground pepper
- beef casings
- sturdy cotton string, cut in 12" long pieces (Dad used Old Charter® bottle to wrap the string around to measure the proper length.)

Directions:
1. In very large tub, mix all ingredients thoroughly. This takes muscles—find a young volunteer.
2. Fill sausage stuffer with meat mixture. Carefully thread casings onto stuffing tube—do not tear. Tie off the end of the casing with a piece of string.
3. Slowly turn the crank on the sausage press. Someone else should guide the sausage off the tube and

work out any air pockets. The casings should be filled tight, but not bulging. Tie off the sausage every 14"-16" or desired length. Tie the sausage again to form a ring—make sure the knot is tight or sausage will fall off the rod during smoking.
4. Carry the sausage to the smoke cellar. Hang on rods. Start fire in corner using hickory wood. Keep fire going until fully smoked, about 15 hours. Sausage can be eaten after it's been smoked but it's plumper and juicier if boiled for about 10 minutes.

Sausage with Apples and Raisins

You can use your favorite variety of sausage with this recipe—brats, smoked sausage, Kielbasa to name a few. Serve with noodles and steamed cabbage.

Serves 4-6

Ingredients:
- 2 pounds sausage
- ½ cup seedless raisins
- 2 apples, sliced but not peeled
- 4 tablespoons butter or margarine
- 2 tablespoons brown sugar

Directions:
1. Melt half the butter in a large skillet, add sausage and fry until browned. Remove from pan.
2. Add raisins, apples and brown sugar and remaining butter. Simmer stirring occasionally until apples are softened.
3. Place sausages on top apple mixture. Cover and simmer 10 minutes.

Bite Size Smokies

Sweet and spicy. Serve with crackers as an appetizer or make a meal with creamed potatoes and stewed red cabbage (recipe page 8) on the side.
Serves 4-6

Ingredients:
- 2 pounds smoked sausage
- 1 cup currant or grape jelly
- 1½ tablespoons mustard (use spicy hot if desired)

Directions:
1. Add jelly and mustard to saucepan. Heat and stir until jelly dissolves. Set aside.
2. Prick smoked sausage in several places. Simmer in water to cover until heated through, about 10-15 minutes. Drain. Cut in ½ inch slices.
3. Place sausage slices in saucepan with jelly mixture cook over low heat. Stir to coat each slice. Serve warm.

Prairie Meals & Memories: Living the Golden Rural

Carolyn Hall

Now that's Crossing the Line

Growing up in Olmitz, I lived in the center of the state. I hadn't crossed the state line until I turned 14 and helped my dad drive to Kansas City to take my Mom to the KU Medical Center for surgery. When I told Dad I expected to see a white line painted on the ground at the Kansas-Missouri border, he knew he had to educate his youngest. Dad had traveled to many states to buy cattle and machine parts, once even to Chicago to drive back a newly purchased school bus for the high school. He also knew the best German restaurant in the Midwest, Meierhoff's in Kansas City, on the Missouri side, just fifteen minutes from the hospital.

After we got Mom settled into her room, he had a plan.

"Mom's tied up in tests the rest of the day, we're going to lunch." He said.

We headed away from the hospital and Dad pulled over on the side of the street just before the intersection.

"See any white line here?" he asked and pointed up to the street sign that read, State Line Road.

This made me an official world traveler, I thought when we started up again and crossed into Missouri. We dined at Meierhoffs, my first venture into a fancy big city restaurant.

"Just one rule," Dad said. "Order something you can't eat at home."

Even though it was lunchtime, the only light at our table came from the flickering candle between us, and what little filtered through nearby stained glass windows.

"Maybe they don't want you to see what they're feeding you." Dad joked, but we managed to make out the menu.

A lot of the food sounded familiar until I came to schnitzel.

"It's breaded and fried veal or pork." Dad explained.

I'd never eaten veal, so we decided that would be a good choice.

"May I take your order, Ma'am," The waiter inquired. "Ma'am?"

But I couldn't answer. For the first time in my life I couldn't talk, my mouth stood wide open and froze. My eyes squinted in the dim light and focused on a couple sitting next to us. I hadn't noticed them until I'd looked up at the waiter.

"That's who you think it is," The waiter said, when he saw me staring at them. "They're here to star in a play at Starlight Theater."

"What's the fuss?" dad asked.

I leaned close and whispered, "Tab Hunter and Gretchen Wilder are sitting right next to us."

"You know somebody in Kansas City?"

"No. They're movie stars." I said.

"Oh." He replied. Dad never went to the shows at the

Great Bend drive-in. Eating lunch so we could get back to Mom took center stage for him.

I enjoyed my schnitzel and made sure to dab any drool over the blond heartthrob on my linen napkin. They left before we finished and without an autograph for Tab's biggest fan. I was shy and Dad didn't think you should interrupt strangers while they enjoyed their meal. But later I did glue the two sugar packets and paper cocktail napkin I retrieved from their table into my scrapbook.

Mom hadn't finished her tests when we returned, so Dad and I talked with someone at the medical center about finding me a room at a local boarding house within walking distance of the hospital. I'd be staying in Kansas City to keep Mom company during her recovery while Dad headed back to start the wheat harvest. At fourteen, I'd be the least helpful with driving the combine and wheat trucks.

I never crossed the state line again that summer. Mom survived being one of what she called 'guinea pigs' for a new procedure to clean out her clogged carotid arteries. She'd suffered two strokes in the past and recovered. This surgery would put a stop to any more we hoped, and as years proved out, it did.

"We're both going home new women," Mom said. I've got a new lease on life and you've made it to Missouri."

The platform, the big portion on the front of a combine, holds the swather (it looks like a riverboat paddle wheel on the front of a combine) which pushes the stands of wheat into the cutting blades. It has to be raised and lowered to meet the lay of the land. The first time I took the wheel of the combine, I didn't have this bit of information and I shaved off the top of a small rise in the wheat field. It sent a cloud of dust out the backside of the combine visible for miles. There's no hiding your mistakes in the wide open prairies and I heard all about it at supper that night.

Jager Schnitzel

All schnitzels are prepared the same, the difference is in the toppings. Weiner schnitzel comes with fresh lemon slices, Schnitzel a la Holstein has a fried egg on top, and my favorite, Jager Schnitzel, meaning Hunter's Schnitzel, has a sauce of mushrooms and onions. Veal, pork or chicken all work well in the recipe. I prefer the pork. Using a mixture of ½ oil and ½ butter allows for the buttery taste but doesn't burn as easily. Put it between a bun and you have an American fried pork tenderloin.
Serves 4

Ingredients:
- 1 pound large, thin slices of pork loin
- 1 cup flour
- salt and pepper to taste
- 1 egg
- 2 teaspoons water
- 1 cup dried breadcrumbs, ground fine
- butter and oil for frying

Topping:
- 1 large onion, chopped fine
- 1 cup fresh mushrooms, sliced
- ¼ cup butter

Directions:
1. Pound meat to a thickness of ⅛" being careful not to tear the meat. Sprinkle with salt and pepper. Beat egg and water until well blended.
2. Dredge meat in flour, coating thoroughly. Dip in egg and water mixture. Coat with breadcrumbs.
3. Let stand at room temperature 15 minutes.
4. Add ¼ cup butter to small skillet. Sauté onions and mushrooms until soft. Keep warm.
5. In large skillet, add equal parts butter and oil to ¼" in depth. Heat. Add breaded pork and fry till golden brown on both sides. Turn only 1 time. Do not pierce breading. Serve immediately, covered with onion and mushrooms.

Carolyn Hall

Watch where you're Steppin'

Common sense worked as the currency to earn the respect of farmers. You learned to work the land for food and shelter, fight the elements for their crops and raise hard working families. Foolishness ran contrary to survival on the prairie. You used sound judgment whenever possible.

Mother's favorite piece of advice was always, "You have a good head on your shoulders, use it."
A certain politician should have paid her good money for that information during his campaign for Kansas Governor.

Dad called me late one evening in October.

"We're you watchin' TV just now?" He asked. "Did you see that political advertisement with that man walking through a pasture full of cows? He was starin' straight up at the sky." Dad laughed so hard he had to stop for a minute before he continued. "Any man that doesn't have the common sense to walk through a herd of cattle and watch where he's steppin' shouldn't be governor of Kansas."

Dad had a way of seeing people for what they truly were and so did most of Kansas that year. Some one else sat in the governor's chair after the election.

Homemade Beef Bologna

Great for appetizers, snacks or a quick lunch. Serve with assorted cheeses, crackers and fresh fruit.
Makes 3 rolls

Ingredients:
- 2 pounds hamburger
- 1 cup water
- 2 tablespoons Morton's Tender Quick
- 2 teaspoons liquid smoke
- ¼ teaspoon garlic powder
- ¼ teaspoon onion powder
- pinch of sage if desired

Directions:
1. Mix all ingredients together until well blended.
2. Shape into 3, 2" rolls (pepperoni size) about 8" long.
3. Wrap in plastic wrap and refrigerate 24 hours.
4. Preheat oven to 300º.
5. Remove plastic wrap. Place in shallow baking pan. Bake 1 hour.

Prairie Folklore

During an intense heat wave in the 1950's, attendance in the Kansas House of Representatives was down and as the few members present nodded off, a legislator made an impassioned plea. He wanted to relocate the capitol to the geographic center of Kansas, to serve everyone equally and be a model for the country. The measure nearly passed until someone realized they'd be moving it to Redwing, a town of 1 grain elevator, 1 beer joint and 1 house.

Prairie Meals & Memories: Living the Golden Rural

Fowl Play

Summer days took longer to get to sundown than most others and Fridays were the worst. We couldn't wait to find out the latest perils for the Green Archer or what Francis the Talking Mule might have to say. The traveling movie man brought new adventures on Friday nights to Olmitz. He projected them on a large wood framed screen between the Knights of Columbus Hall and the Civil Defense Tower.

Wooden benches fanned out in rows beneath the screen and families brought blankets for the grass, if you dared to chance the chiggers. Movies and friends served as a good reward for a week's worth of hard work choking down dust and browning in the Kansas sun.

The evening took on a church social atmosphere. The men cleared the equipment out of the city works building and set up grills. The night air hung heavy with the aroma of frying hamburgers. You waited your turn to buy one layered with pickles and onions on a Rainbow bun wrapped in waxed paper. My friend Kathy and I would share a bottle of pop we fished out of the long narrow stock tank filled with ice and Dr. Pepper, Orange and Grape Crush, Chocolate Yahoo and other favorites. You gave your money to the man with a cigar clenched in his teeth wearing, a seed company cap.

When just enough darkness set in to bring the screen to life, the crowd found their seats and hushed the kids. It was show time. Dust particles and the haze of smoke from the grills floated in the air, caught the light of the projector. The two story screen took us beyond our Kansas prairie and showed us a world of excitement and fun.

We'd finished our chores early that Friday. We wanted to get to town ahead of the crowd and secure a good seat. My brother Johnnie couldn't wait for the new episode of his favorite, The Green Archer. I usually played dolls with Kathy until Francis the Talking Mule came on screen. Boy stuff didn't interest me.

We'd changed out of our chore clothes and Mom had me sit on the arm of the divan to braid fresh pigtails in my hair. Johnnie got his Gene Autry Holster and guns just in case his hero needed assistance, and my sisters put on their freshly ironed town clothes and waited for us to finish. That's when we heard a blaring horn from the highway and screeching brakes. A gaggle of our farm geese had followed one another into the path of a car. Mom put on the hot water to boil and the evening festivities moved to the kitchen table. With a quick change of clothes, we all butchered geese till early morning.

Farm life had a way of teaching priorities and sacrifices, but we weathered them together. Roast goose always brings back memories of Francis the Talking Mule. As for my brother Johnnie, he's never forgiven the feathered road kill for missing an episode of his superhero, The Green Archer.

Roast Goose

There's nothing like a meal of roast goose. No wonder old stories talk about having a Christmas goose for holiday dinner. But don't wait for a special occasion to try it.
Serves 6

Ingredients:
- 1 8-pound goose, oven ready
- 4 onions, quartered
- 4 tart apples, quartered
- 4 stalks of celery, cut in chunks
- 1 quart hot water
- 2 cloves
- 1 bay leaf
- 1 cup apple butter

Directions:
1. Preheat oven to 325°.
2. Stuff goose with onions, apples and celery, cloves and bay leaf. Place breast side down on rack in roasting pan. Add water. Place in oven.
3. Turn goose after 2 hours. Continue roasting 1 more hour. Remove from pan.
4. Pour pan drippings into saucepan. Let cool slightly. Skim off excess fat. Bring to boil and thicken with apple butter.
5. Carve the goose. Chop the stuffing and use for chutney. Serve the sauce warm, on the side.

Prairie Know-How
After plucking the feathers from a duck, melt paraffin and dip the duck in the melted wax. Cool. After paraffin sets up, pull it off and it takes off the down and pin feathers with it.

Chicken Stew

Serve this over biscuits or in a soup bowl with some fresh baked bread on the side. A great way to use leftover chicken, turkey or quail. If you don't have leftovers, bake 2 chicken breasts at 375° for 20 minutes sprinkled with ½ teaspoon poultry seasoning.
Serves 6

Ingredients:

- 2 cups frozen peas
- 2 cups diced carrots
- 1 medium onion, chopped
- ½ cup celery, chopped
- ½ cup mushrooms, chopped
- ¼ cup butter or margarine
- ⅓ cup flour
- ½ teaspoon salt
- ½ teaspoon ground sage
- ½ poultry seasoning
- ¼ teaspoon tarragon
- 2 tablespoons dried parsley
- dash nutmeg
- ¼ teaspoon pepper
- 2 cups water
- ¾ cup milk
- 1 tablespoon chicken base or instant bouillon granules
- 2 cups cubed cooked chicken (meat lovers may want 3 cups)

Directions:

1. Combine peas and carrots and cook according to package directions for peas.
2. In large saucepan, cook onions, celery and mushrooms in butter till tender. Stir in flour, salt, sage, poultry seasoning, pepper, parsley and nutmeg until dissolved. Add water, milk, and chicken base.

Cook and stir until thick and bubbly.
3. Stir in drained, cooked peas and carrots, and cooked chicken. Simmer over medium heat 10-15 minutes, stirring constantly.

Civil Defense Shelters in the 1950's
All the small Kansas towns in the area had Civil Defense Towers. Locals, including Boy Scout troops, received training in spotting enemy aircraft. Our town folded up the lower steps to prevent youngsters from playing in the tower, but we climbed the supports to the next landing and found ourselves in the middle of the cold war. At the top of the tower, we found photographs of American and Russian planes used for identification purposes. We played under and around the tower, never grasping the severity of its mission to keep America safe.

Prairie Meals & Memories: Living the Golden Rural

Carolyn Hall

No Empty Nest

We raised a lot of chickens on our farm. Dad bought the baby chicks from the hatchery instead of getting them the old fashioned way. In earlier times, Grandma used setting hens to hatch the chicks. She waited for a hen to "go broody" which meant the chicken would show signs of being in the mood for motherhood. The hen would stay on her eggs, even at night, and become protective of her nest. She instinctively hid her eggs from predators and threatened with a loud squawk or a sharp peck if she got disturbed.

We sold eggs to the grocery store in town and had no need for setting hens. Grandma worked to discourage the feathered ladies when she gathered their eggs twice a day. Unfortunately, now that I was tall enough to reach the nests, gathering eggs became my job.

"Don't let those setting hens keep you from getting all the eggs," Grandma reminded me.

My hand still had the bruise from my last encounter with one of those protective old biddies. She'd pecked me so fast, I didn't have a chance. I borrowed my older brother's water pistol and hid it in the elastic waist band of my shorts. Grandma thought harassing her chickens would stunt their egg laying ability. I had to be careful.

With the wire egg basket in hand, I headed to the chicken house. I worked my way through the hens scratching in the dirt outside the door. The first row of nests had only eggs on the straw inside but the two-story metal nests had one mean-eyed, needing to be chicken fried hen. She pulled her head back ready for attack and growled a clucking noise at me. I pulled my gun and dowsed her good. I know what the person went through when they originated the phrase, "mad as an old wet hen". She craned her neck out as far as she could, throwing her beak at me. She ruffled her feathers and squawked so loud the few chickens in the henhouse ran for the door. But she didn't get off the eggs.

I couldn't leave without them. Last month, Grandma had been down sick for over a week and I'd let the setting hen keep her dumb eggs. When Grandma gathered the rotten eggs from underneath the hen, it was me that didn't do any sitting for a while.

This meant drastic measures. I finished getting the eggs from all the open nests and put the basket up for safe keeping. I found an old 2x4 Dad used to prop open one of the windows in the heat of the summer. I pounded on the metal side of the nest. She didn't budge.

It would be supper soon. I paced back and forth in front of the nest, under constant surveillance of the beady-eyed chicken. There had to be a way to get those eggs. I ran to Dad's workshop and found his welding gloves—that hard pointed beak couldn't hurt me now.

With a grin on my face and leather gloves up to my

armpits, I picked up the 2x4 and pushed it under the feathered fiend. As I pried her up she pecked and scolded me.

"What do you think you're doing?" Grandma asked.
I dropped the board and froze.

"You'll break more eggs than you'll get. That poor hen probably won't lay for a week now."
I watched as Grandma faced down the chicken. She took one hand and gently pushed the protesting hen's head against the side of nest and reached under the feathered bottom and retrieved the eggs, one at a time. They came out cracked after the encounter with the 2x4.

"Now, was that so hard?" She asked.
I picked up the wire basket while she carried the shattered eggs in her hands. We walked in silence back to the house. I ate scrambled eggs for supper.

Next time I gathered eggs, I learned from Grandma's trick. It only takes one gloved hand to hold the chicken's head against the nest. I got under and out with no cracks or pecks and only a few ruffled feathers.

Savory Roast Chicken

This could be a tasty finish to a cranky old setting hen, but a broiler-fryer chicken works well too. The aroma while this dish roasts is mouth watering. If neatness counts, you can put the mixed pickling spices in a cheesecloth bag before inserting into chicken cavity. Surround the chicken with new potatoes and unpeeled garlic cloves while it bakes. Using your fingers, squeeze the roasted garlic from its jacket and use as a spread on warmed bread with your meal. Add maple glazed carrots (recipe on page 6) for a spectacular Sunday dinner.
Serves 5-6

Ingredients:
- ¼ cup oil
- 1 2½-3 pound chicken
- 1 tablespoon butter or margarine
- 1 tablespoon mixed pickling spices
- 1 bay leaf
- salt and pepper to taste
- 2 pounds whole new potatoes, scrubbed, not peeled (about 12-14)
- 30-40 cloves garlic, unpeeled (3+ large heads)

Directions:
1. Preheat oven to 375°.
2. Pour 2 tablespoons of oil in roasting pan.
3. Rinse chicken inside and out. Pat dry. Sprinkle salt and pepper in cavity. Add butter, bay leaf and mixed pickling spices. Place chicken breast side up in roasting pan.

4. Place potatoes and garlic around the chicken. Sprinkle potatoes with additional salt and pepper. Drizzle chicken and potatoes with the remaining oil.
5. Roast uncovered for 10 minutes. Reduce heat to 350° and continue roasting 60-70 minutes or until chicken is no longer pink. Turn potatoes occasionally to crisp evenly.

Hot Mamas

After enjoying a jar of store-bought hot sausages (a 32 ounce jar or larger), my brother Johnnie saves the jar and liquid and refills the jar with hardboiled eggs. Serve these for appetizers or with sandwiches. They can also jazz up a bland egg salad.
Makes: one jar of hot spiced eggs

Ingredients:
- Reserved liquid from hot spiced sausages
- Hard boiled eggs—amount depends on size of jar

Directions:
1. Remove shells from eggs.
2. Place in original jar from sausages. Pour reserved liquid over eggs, making sure at least 1" of liquid remains above top layer of eggs. Refrigerate.

Never Fail Meringue

You'll find this different twist on meringue to be an easy success. It'll make your guests think your pie came from a fancy bakery, but then it did—yours. This meringue clings tight to the pie crust after it's baked, doesn't turn watery and refrigerates well.

Makes: enough to top 1 pie

Ingredients:
- ½ cup water
- 1 tablespoon cornstarch
- 3 large egg whites, or about ½ cup, room temperature
- 6 tablespoons sugar
- 1 teaspoon vanilla

Directions:
1. Preheat oven to 350°.
2. In small saucepan, combine water and cornstarch over medium high heat, stirring constantly. Boil till transparent and glossy. Cool slightly.
3. In large mixing bowl, add egg whites, sugar, vanilla and cornstarch mixture. With electric mixer, beat on high until stiff peaks form.
4. Spread on cream pie. Use knife to form peaks and swirls on top of meringue.
5. Bake 20-25 minutes until peaks turn golden. Do not brown. Cool and serve.

Prairie Humor

A New Jersey city slicker moved to Kansas in hopes of becoming a chicken farmer. He went to the local hatchery and bought several crates of baby chicks. One week later he came back and ordered another batch of chicks.

"Back for more? the salesman said. "You must be doing a great job with your chicks."

"No, I lost every last one of those you sold me last week."

"Sorry to hear it, what went wrong?"

"Forgot to ask—was I supposed to plant them beak up?"

Prairie Superstition

Tie a red rag around a hen's neck. She may fuss about it, but she'll never think of setting again.

Prairie Meals & Memories: Living the Golden Rural

Carolyn Hall

Hang 'em High

Farmers invented recycling. Early settlers on the prairie burned dried buffalo manure and later cow manure known as 'chips' for heat and cooking. We mended fences with the bailing wire left over from feeding bailed hay to the cows, and we saved our bath water for the next in line on bath night.

Dad even found a use for the old doubletrees from his draft horse farming days. He took the wooden shaft that held a metal hook on each end and attached it to a winch. On butchering day, he'd use it to pull the animal carcass into a tall tree to drain the blood and keep it safe from the dogs.

Temptation overcame my brother when the butchering crew took their lunch break before they removed the contraption from the tree.

"Want to go for a ride?" Johnnie asked, looking up into the tree.

"What do I have to do?" I asked.

"Just grab onto the doubletree and I'll pull you up. It'll be fun." He said. "You're not a fraidy cat are you?"

"Course not. You won't let me fall, will you?"

"Just hold on tight. Hurry up before they're done eating." I grabbed on and up I went.

"I want down now, Johnnie. Johnnie? Johnnnnnieeee!"

He'd vanished. All I could see was the rope he'd pulled me up with tied to the bumper of the old Chevy pick-up.

It didn't take long for my screams to bring a crowd. Dad got me down, but Johnnie didn't sit down for a while.

Singletrees and doubletrees:
Pivoting wooden swing bars with a hook on each end that attached to a working horse's harness and enabled them to draw a load. A singletree for one horse and a doubletree balanced the load between two. Today they can be found suspended in flower gardens holding a hanging basket on each end.
Sidebar:

My dream of having a horse ended when Mom said, "Your dad said he'd never have another horse on the farm after he bought a tractor. He'd plowed behind them for so many years, he never wanted to look at the working end of a horse again."

I improvised and learned to ride one of my pet calves. I rode bare back and bare footed. When he got tired of me 'horsing' around, he'd head for the biggest road thorn patch and waited for me to give up. I finally climbed off—very carefully.

Pickled Pigs Feet

Farmers don't let anything go to waste. Mom always said when we butchered a pig we used everything but the squeal. Some call this recipe zitter or souse. Make this in a 6- quart slow cooker. Be sure and clean the shanks well. Skin them and make sure no hog hairs remain. You might want to make this when you can open a window or two, the aroma will open your sinuses. Best not to surprise your city husband with a cracker full without warning, pickled pigs feet can be an acquired taste. Serve with assorted crackers.
Makes: 1 large container

Ingredients:

- 4 medium fresh pork shanks, not hocks, a little higher up the leg
- 3 cured or smoked hocks
- salt
- water
- 1 package Knox ® gelatin
- 4-5 tablespoons vinegar
- 1 tablespoon mixed pickling spices
- 3 onions, sliced thin

Directions:
1. In large bowl, cover fresh shanks and cured hocks with water, add 2 tablespoons salt. Cover container and refrigerate 2 days.
2. Remove from salt water and trim all visible fat from cured hocks. Place shanks and hocks in slow cooker. Add mixed pickling spices and 1 onion. Cook on low heat 8 hours.
3. Remove from slow cooker and cool to lukewarm. Strain juice. Let set and skim off fat.
4. Cut meat from bone. Use only the lean meat and place in 10"x 8" pan.

5. Pour juice into saucepan. Bring to boil. Add vinegar, Knox gelatin, salt to taste and remaining 2 sliced onions.
6. Pour over meat. Refrigerate until gelatin sets up. Serve cold. Remove any fat from top before serving.

Prairie Superstition
Bite down on a piece of bread crust to stop the tears when peeling an onion.

Harvest Hand Pot Roast

Bay leaves and lots of garlic add a bold taste of Germany to this family favorite. Leftovers make a great start for vegetable beef soup. Try making it in a pressure cooker, and cut your cooking time by more than half. Follow the instructions in your manual for Beef Pot Roast. When pressure has completely dropped, remove the meat and strain off pan drippings and save. Add carrots and potatoes and follow manual instructions for amount of liquid to add for cooking of fresh vegetables, cook 8 minutes. Use the pan drippings to make the roast gravy (recipe on page 181).
Serves 6

Ingredients:

- 2 tablespoons oil
- 3 to 4 pounds beef chuck or arm roast
- 2 large onions, quartered
- 1 cup celery, cut into 1" slices
- ½ cup red wine
- 2 tablespoons Kitchen Bouquet ®
- 3 cups water
- 2 bay leaves
- 2 teaspoons seasoning salt
- 5 peppercorns
- 1 tablespoon Worcestershire sauce
- 1 tablespoon soy sauce
- 5 cloves garlic
- 2 cups baby carrots
- 6 medium potatoes, peeled and quartered

Directions:
1. Preheat oven to 325°
2. Heat oil in skillet. Add meat and brown on all sides. Place in roaster. Add remaining ingredients

except for carrots and potatoes. Cover. Bake 2 hours.
3. Remove from oven. Add carrots and potatoes. Return to oven and bake an additional 1 hour or until meat is tender. Reserve pan drippings for gravy.

Pot Roast Gravy

Don't let your roast beef and potatoes go bare, cover them with this hearty gravy. Be sure and serve bread with the meal, you'll want to use it to soak up every drop.

Ingredients:
- 2½-3 cups pan juices (add a little water if necessary)
- 1 teaspoon Kitchen Bouquet ®
- 1 teaspoon Worcestershire sauce
- 1 teaspoon soy sauce
- 3 tablespoons cornstarch
- ½ cup water

Directions:
1. Bring pan juices to rolling boil in saucepan. Reduce heat and let cook 10 minutes. Add Kitchen Bouquet ®, Worcestershire and soy sauce.
2. Dissolve cornstarch in water and pour into hot mixture, stirring constantly. Continue cooking and stirring over high medium heat until well thickened. Serve hot.

Prairie Home Remedy
If you stepped on a rusty nail, you packed your foot in fresh cow manure. You used the same treatment for a bee sting.

Prairie Meals & Memories: Living the Golden Rural

Cumshawed

You grew up under everyone's eyes in the country—God's, Grandma's, and neighbors', but who would suspect the Pizza Hut manager?

Nothing spells trouble like a group of teenagers with a car, a little cash and Saturday night. We'd just finished a successful run of our senior play, two nights of packing them into the high school gym. Actually, after the first 75 seats got set up, the janitor just unfolded chairs as people trickled in—no empty spaces at our performances.

Most of our class, 18 in total, had starring roles. With 116 in our four-year school, we were the smallest class and always up for an adventure. We decided we needed to do something special to celebrate our final curtain call.

"Let's get a pizza," Susie hollered.

We piled more than the legal limit in a few cars and headed toward Great Bend, the big city, population 10,000 more or less, 25 miles away. Growing up, fast food usually meant lunch meat sandwiches, but Griff's Burger Bar and Pizza Hut had invaded Great Bend and we were hooked.

Of course, you couldn't just leave town quietly, you had to drag Main Street first. Otis, home to our fighting Eagles of Otis High School, had it's own designated route. One car took the lead, and the others fell in line and followed each others' tail lights in a mindless procession back and forth from just past the bank to Steiben's Garage and back again. Horns blared, and arms flailed from open windows as the parade met itself on the U-turns.

When we got tired of playing follow the leader, we headed to 96 highway and on to Great Bend. At the Pizza Hut, we crowded around a couple of tables we'd put together in the corner. We were out-of-town kids and didn't know anyone else in the new "hang-out". That didn't bother us because we were seniors and seniors are cool no matter where they're from.

We'd drained our cokes and finished off the last slices of pepperoni and supreme pizzas.

"You know, they say the cool thing to do is see if you can smuggle out one of the cheese shakers when you leave," one of the guys said and looked straight at me. "Bet you can't." He picked up the glass jar full of Parmesan on our table and shook it at me.

"I don't need a cheese shaker." I said. Grandma and the nuns at St. Ann's instilled a conscience in me so loud I just knew other people heard it shouting in my ear. Today I would've been called a nerd, back then I was a sissy.

"Come on, nobody even knows you in here," another voice chimed in. "There's one on every table. Bet they got dozens. Take it to remember your senior year." And then came the shot to the heart, "You're not chicken are you?"

Yes I was. But to strike out against my fear and to defy

those saintly voices in my head, and in a move of out and out stupidity, I put the darned thing in my purse.

The next morning at church, I realized I still had what my brother-in-law Gary would've called the 'cumshawed' item in my purse.

"When somebody takes something they don't intend to return, they call it cumshawed. In the service, they called it a midnight requisition, kind of a bonus you gave yourself. Doesn't sound as bad that way." He'd explained. "Like picking a trunk load of a farmer's corn 'cause he's got a whole field of it anyway."

It sure didn't feel like a bonus to me. I just wanted to throw it away. But then my conscience reminded me that would be a waste.

After church, my sister, Ronnie and her husband Gary came for a visit. They lived in Great Bend.

"My friend Jim thinks you and I look a lot alike." Ronnie said. I could see one of her eyebrows raised and she looked like she wanted to ask me a question. But she didn't get a chance. Gary started giggling and shaking his head.

"What's so funny about us looking alike?" I asked.

"He said he saw you at the Pizza Hut last night and knew you had to be my little sister." Ronnie said. "Especially since the guy beside you had on his Otis letter jacket."

"Pizza Hut?" I asked. My ears burned red.

"Yah. He's the manager. Jim said to tell you whenever you're finished with his cheese shaker, he'd like to have it back."

Prairie Wisdom
God loved the prairie so much he didn't see fit to hide it under trees.

Homemade Pizza

I made a few homemade pizzas before I had the nerve to return to the Pizza Hut. Lucky for me refrigerator rolls became the new sensation to try and these crescent rolls made easy pizza bread. Serve with a wilted lettuce salad (recipe on page 4). Use your own parmesan cheese shaker to spread the cheese.
Serves 6

Ingredients:
- 1 tube crescent rolls (8 rolls)
- 2 tablespoons butter, margarine, melted or olive oil
- 1 teaspoon dried basil
- 1 teaspoon garlic powder
- 1 15-ounce can pizza sauce (about 2 cups)
- 24-36 slices of pepperoni
- 1 cup shredded mozzarella Cheese
- ½ cup parmesan cheese

Directions:
1. Preheat oven to 375°.
2. Unroll crescent dough onto greased baking sheet. Press into 12"x 9" rectangle, seal seams. Brush with butter or oil, sprinkle with spices. Bake 10 minutes.
3. Remove from oven, spread evenly with pizza sauce. Top with pepperoni and mozzarella cheese. Bake 10 minutes longer or until crust turns golden brown.
4. Spread parmesan evenly over pizza. Cut into 6 slices.

The Pizza Hut Restaurants originated in Wichita, Kansas in 1958.

Prairie Meals & Memories: Living the Golden Rural

Carolyn Hall

Scaredy Cats

There's not much shade in Central Kansas from the hot July sun. Infrequent tree lined creeks and rivers provided water, food and recreation for those lucky enough to live nearby. Kids gathered at the creek banks to escape the summer heat, an oasis on the prairie. Here, cottonwoods grew to towering heights supported by trunks you couldn't reach your arms around. The giant trees clung to the banks for moisture and their roots reached out like gnarled fingers on the edge of the water. The kids sat on the roots, dangled their feet into the creek and hoped nothing unseen would nibble their toes.

Summer gulley washers brought rains that caused rivers to swell and spill their currents into normally docile creeks. The roiling muddy water carried with it dirt, debris and large fish, especially large flathead catfish. These bottom feeders were fattened in the large rivers, the likes of the Kansas River known to locals as the Kaw, the Arkansas River and the Smoky Hill.

When the water levels dropped, the big cats found themselves stranded in the unfamiliar shallow creek beds. The sand bars left in the middle of the water, formed deeper pools along the banks and harbored the marooned fish.

After the creeks calmed down, it was time for a wet adventure. Splashing in the sun warmed water, looking for crawdad holes and clam shells made for a fun afternoon. We had to travel over a mile to get to a creek, but my sister's friend Joy lived near Blood Creek. Rose couldn't wait to spend the weekend with her friend Joy and get away from pesky siblings.

When the thermometer passed 100°, they headed for the creek. They wore old shorts and shirts to play in the brown water. They saved their swimming suits for the chlorinated community pool in town.

Their quiet afternoon of play ended when a bunch of local boys, idled by muddy farm fields, decided to go 'noodling' for catfish. The ample supply of stranded flatheads meant easy marks for the fried fish loving crowd. A 'noodler' would crawl into the creek, find their prey and pat the top of the fish's head to reassure the finned critter. They'd work their hand into the cat's mouth and push the body of the fish into the soft creek mud under the bank, and 'catch' their supper. Next, they'd flip the fish onto the bank and someone else slipped it into a gunny sack to carry home.

The boys' fun hadn't ended yet. They noticed my sister and her friend watching their escapades and decided to liven up the afternoon. They selected one of their largest catfish and chased the girls down the creek bank, into the pasture and all the way to Joy's house.

Joy's Mother, Beulah, heard terrified screams and ran outside to help. Rose and Joy jumped on the porch and took refuge behind Beulah. The red faced boys decided a good-sized flathead cat made for a much needed peace offering and traded a sound scolding for supper.

More than 50 years later, after my sister Rose welcomed her son, Brent, home from a tour in Iraq, he shared his experiences with her.

"Mom, they have a strange way of fishing over there." He said. "During a break, we sat and watched them along the river. Would you believe they got in the water, trapped the fish next to the bank, stuck their hand in the fish's mouth and flipped it out onto the bank?"

"Son, that's called noodling. I've eaten some good sized catfish that came out of Blood Creek the same way."

 **It's illegal to use a bathtub to hand fish for flathead catfish in Kansas.**

Prairie Wisdom
Be sure you've 'noodled' a catfish not a snapping turtle or your friends might call you 'nubbins'.

'Draws' have three vital definitions on the prairie:
- A beer on tap at a tavern
- What Hop-along Cassidy did with his guns to stop the bad guys
- Waterways cut by erosion that run through the flatlands and carry water after torrential rains known as gully washers

Prairie Folklore
When the waters ran red from the fierce battles of the Indians Wars, the locals named the creek, Blood Creek.

Beer Battered Catfish with Dill Dipping Sauce

The key to this recipe is having all the ingredients cold before you start. To liven this up you can add 1 teaspoon Cajun seasoning—more if you dare. Mix the batter just before you intend to use it or it will lose its punch.
Makes 6 fillets

Ingredients:
- 6 catfish fillets or the catch of the day
- 1 cup Bisquick ®
- 1 cup cornmeal
- 2 medium eggs, beaten
- ½ cup flour
- 1 12-ounce can beer
- 1 teaspoon garlic powder
- 1 teaspoon onion powder
- oil for deep frying

Directions:
1. Preheat oil in deep skillet or deep fryer to 325°
2. Pat fillets dry with paper towel.
3. Mix the cornmeal, Bisquick ®, and seasonings together. Add eggs then stir in beer.
4. Dip fillets into batter and deep fry fish until golden brown, about 4-5 minutes.

Dill Dip

This creamy dip goes great with just about anything from fried fish to garden fresh vegetables. Refrigerate overnight for maximum taste. Do not substitute dill seed for the dill weed.
Makes 2 cups

Ingredients:
- 1 cup sour cream
- 1 cup real mayonnaise
- 2 tablespoons dill weed
- 2 teaspoons seasoning salt
- 2 tablespoons minced dried onion or 1 teaspoon onion powder

Directions:
1. Combine all ingredients in mixing bowl. Beat on medium speed until thoroughly blended.
2. Chill at least 1 hour before serving.

Broiled Perch in Lemon Sauce

You'll be heading back to catch another stringer-full for seconds of this lemony dish. White wine or cooking sherry can be used, they each give a little different flavor to the sauce. Be sure and make the sauce before you start the fish. Serve with rice, fresh asparagus and frosted cherry apple pie for dessert (recipe on page 23).
Serves 4

Ingredients:
- 4 large perch fillets
- *Lemon Sauce:*
- ½ cup honey
- ½ cup water
- ¼ cup rice vinegar
- ¼ cup white wine or sherry
- 1 tablespoon cornstarch
- 1 tablespoon minced garlic or 1 teaspoon granulated garlic
- 1 fresh lemon, sliced
- 1 tablespoon grated lemon peel

Directions:
Sauce:
1. Combine all ingredients except the lemon slices in a small saucepan. Over medium heat, bring to a boil and stir constantly until thickened. Reduce heat. Add lemon slices, simmer 5 minutes. Keep warm.
2. Allow 4-6 minutes of broiling time per ½" thickness of fillet. Broil 3"-4" from heat source until fish flakes easily. Or use a dual sided indoor grill according to manufacturer's instructions.
3. Arrange fish in shallow serving pan. Cover with lemon sauce.

Prairie Meals & Memories: Living the Golden Rural

Bayrischer Style Crappie

The bay leaf gives this a rich flavor. Serve with potato pancakes (page 3) and stewed red cabbage (page 8). Serves 6

Ingredients:
- 3 pounds crappie fillets
- ⅓ cup butter or margarine
- ¾ cup onions, chopped
- 1 bay leaf
- ¼ teaspoon thyme
- 1 clove garlic, minced
- salt and pepper to taste

Garnish:
- parsley flakes
- lemon wedges

Directions:
1. Preheat oven to 350°
2. Line greased baking pan with onions, sprinkle with garlic and thyme. Add bay leaf.
3. Season crappie with salt and pepper. Dot with butter. Place on top onion mixture and cover.
4. Bake for 25-30 minutes. Baste twice.
5. Reserve sauce from baking pan and serve with fish. Garnish with parsley and lemon wedges.

Carolyn Hall

Game

Prairie Meals & Memories: Living the Golden Rural

Carolyn Hall

You Need a Permit for That Ma'am

My friend Shannon had more encounters with whitetails than the average hunter. Unfortunately, she found them on the highway on her way to work at 6 a.m., not in the serenity of the woods. She lost the front end to her car twice and the third deer tried to jump through her driver's side window, all in just a few months time.

"I'm getting gun shy about driving to work," she told her husband Bill.

"Thank God you haven't been hurt." He said racking up brownie points. "But if you're keeping score, you've killed three of them." Husbands never know to quit when they're in positive territory.

Bill came in after work the next week with the mail in hand. "You've got a letter from the state."

"Probably an early birthday reminder from Kansas. My driver's license comes due this year." She said.

"Your renewal, huh?"

"Yep."

When she got home from work the next day, Bill handed her a letter from the Kansas Wildlife Biologist.

"Looks like you've got another letter from the state. You're getting pretty popular." He handed her the envelope and waited for her to open it.

What's the wildlife biologist want with me?" she asked.

"What? You won't believe this, Bill." Her voice raised an octave. "Kansas wants me to get a gosh dang hunting license before they'll give me a new driver's license. Listen to this," she said and read him the letter.

Dear Mrs. Armstrong,
It has come to our attention that your driver's license is up for renewal. We have been notified that you have been involved in vehicular accidents that resulted in the deaths of three Kansas deer in the past year. In Kansas, there is a state policy that requires anyone who has killed three or more deer with their motor vehicle to first apply for a deer hunting permit before they can renew their driver's license.
Enclosed is the permit application. Please fill it out and return to this office for processing. When your application has been approved, we will notify the driver's license bureau of your compliance.
Sincerely,
John Smith, Kansas State Wildlife Biologist

"That's the dumbest thing I've heard. I didn't go out looking for the critters, they found me."

"Suppose they'll issue you a special license, maybe take your picture in camouflage?"

"Not funny." She said and started rifling through the telephone book.

"Who you gonna call?" Bill asked.

"The governor's office. I want to know why the state's wasting my money on stuff like this." She marked the number with her finger and reached for the phone. "That wildlife biologist has some explaining to do."

"You sure you want to do that? He's just doing his job."

"And I need my driver's license for my job."

"You know how you said you didn't want to hit any more deer?"

"Yah? So what does that have to do with this?"

"Well, this dear doesn't want to get hit when he tells you he made up that letter and sent it to you."

Skillet Venison Leavenworth Style

This one-pot meal will warm the heart of the victorious hunter back from his lonely cold days in a tree stand. Serve over extra wide noodles with a side of biscuits.
Serves 4

Ingredients:
- 1 pound venison steaks, see sidebar
- 1 large onion, sliced thin
- 1 green pepper, sliced thin
- paprika and garlic powder to taste
- salt and pepper to taste
- 1 cup Italian style bread crumbs
- butter for frying
- olive oil
- Worcestershire sauce
- 1 can tomatoes (16 ounce size)
- 1 can green beans, (16 ounce size), drained (optional)

Directions:
1. Heat butter in large skillet. Sauté onion and green pepper. Set aside.
2. Season steak to taste with garlic, paprika, salt and pepper. Coat with bread crumbs. Brown each side 4-5 minutes in butter with a splash of olive oil and Worcestershire sauce.
3. Add onion and green pepper back to skillet, place over steak. Pour can of tomatoes with liquid over steak. Cover and simmer 45 minutes to 1 hour until tender.
4. Add green beans, drained. Simmer until beans are tender.

Prairie Tip
How to cook venison:
- Remove all fat, sinew (tough fibrous tissue connecting bone to muscle) and bone from the meat to prevent *gamey* taste.
- Butter enhances the taste
- Do not over-cook while browning
- Wild game steaks are best served rare to medium rare

Deer 'n Coke ®

Old fashioned fried steak with a modern marinade. Make the cream gravy to smother the steak and mashed potatoes. Add fresh sliced tomatoes and corn on the cob and you're heaven bound.
Serves 4-6

Ingredients:
- 2 pounds of venison steaks, cut into serving size portions
- 1 12-ounce can Coke ®, not diet
- 1 cup flour
- ½ teaspoon garlic powder
- ½ teaspoon seasoning salt
- salt and pepper to taste
- oil and butter for frying

Gravy:
- 2 tablespoons flour
- 2½-2¾ cup milk
- salt and pepper to taste

Directions:
1. Place steak in large plastic storage bag. Add Coke ® and seal bag. Refrigerate 24 hours, turning bag several times for equal marinating.
2. Drain. Mix flour and spices together. Dredge meat in flour mixture. Fry in mixture of half oil and half butter until done.

3. In same skillet, pour off all but 2 tablespoons of oil mixture from frying steak. Add 2 tablespoons flour to hot oil mixture and stir until well blended and flour browns. Add milk. Stir continuously until gravy thickens. Add salt and pepper to taste.

Buffalo & Beef Meatballs

These small meatballs with a hint of chili powder bathed in barbecue sauce will be great at your next tailgate party. Serve as an appetizer or a hot sandwich on a toasted hoagie bun. Can bake, freeze then reheat these.
Makes two 9"x13" pans full

Ingredients:
- 2 eggs, beaten
- 1 can evaporated milk (13 ounce size)
- 2 cups quick oatmeal
- 1 cup onion, chopped fine
- 1 tablespoon, garlic minced
- 2 teaspoons salt
- 1 teaspoon pepper
- 2 teaspoons chili powder
- 1½ pounds lean hamburger
- 1½ pounds ground buffalo

Sauce:
- 2 cups ketchup
- 1½ pounds cups brown sugar
- 2 tablespoons liquid smoke
- 1 tablespoon garlic, minced
- ½ cup onion, chopped fine

Directions:
1. Preheat oven to 350°.
2. Combine all ingredients except meats and mix well. Add meats and mix well by hand.
3. Shape into walnut size balls. Place in 2 greased 9"x13" pans.

Sauce:
4. Blend all ingredients until dissolved and pour half of sauce into each pan to cover meatballs.
5. Bake 50-60 minutes.

There's more meatballs in this recipe than the number of buffalo in Central Kansas when I grew up on the prairie. I saw my first buffalo in a zoo. Decades later, I lived close to a herd for several years in Shawnee, Kansas, where I raised my family.

Pastures in Kansas have many large recesses called 'buffalo wallows'. Buffalos used to roll in the dust or sometimes the mud and left deep depressions in the landscapes. You could lose a pickup axle to one of these if you weren't paying attention.

Prairie Wisdom
Mom learned to drive a car while horse drawn wagons shared the road. When I learned to drive, she told me her dad warned her never to drive on the shoulder of the road. "You'll pick up all the nails in your tires. They work loose from the wagons and roll to the side of the road."

Carolyn Hall

Snipe Hunting in Snipes Hollow

Practical jokes made life on the prairie a lot more fun, unless you ended up on the receiving end a few too many times. We'd heard the stories of sending people on wild goose chases trying to catch a snipe. Our pasture, aptly nicknamed Snipes Hollow, had seen its share of pranksters.

A group of so-called friends would invite a novice, usually a town kid, to go snipe hunting. They'd wait for a moonless night and head out to Snipes Hollow. The unwitting soul got stationed in one end of the pasture and told to hold a gunny sack open and close to the ground.

"We'll head off over near the cedars and shoo the birds your direction." He'd be told.

I never knew the longest time anyone waited before they figured out they'd been 'sniped', but I heard jokes about how someone fell asleep waiting to fill their gunny sack.

It came as quite a surprise to everyone when my sister and one of her friends found an injured bird in Snipes Hollow and it turned out to be a real snipe.

Our farm is only 10 miles from Cheyenne Bottoms, a major bird refuge. Turns out people had been looking for snipes in the wrong pasture. They nested in the grasslands at the Bottoms. Our snipe had gotten a little off course from Cheyenne Bottoms. Turns out snipes pass through there quite often.

Cheyenne Bottoms, known as the Jewel of the Prairie, a 41,000-acre lowland just outside Great Bend, is the largest interior marsh in the U.S. It's one of the 8 wonders of Kansas with over 320 species of birds recorded.

Flocks of white seagulls follow the farm tractors and scavenge for worms and insects as plows break open fresh ground every summer in Central Kansas.

Prairie Meals & Memories: Living the Golden Rural

Carolyn Hall

Struttin' Their Stuff in the Shelterbelt

After the dust bowl in the 1930's, farmers in Kansas planted rows of trees, called shelterbelts, to protect their homesteads from the dust and snow blown by the relentless prairie winds. Drought tolerant trees lined driveways and landmarked the farms with individual style. I recognized someone's farm more by their tree configuration than their house. Most times, the farmhouses couldn't be seen from the road.

Grandpa had planted elms that now tickled the power lines and fanned out along Number 4 highway to the east from our driveway culvert and plump red cedars marched to the west. Locust and elm led the way on either side of the rutted gravel road to our limestone house.

Depending on which way the wind blew, I'd locate my tea parties on different sides of the house.

"Mom, I wish those trees would stop making the wind blow." I said pulling strands of hair out of my mouth.

"Honey, the trees don't make the wind. My dad planted those trees to slow it down."

"Just like he built the house?" I asked, remembering Mom telling me about our hand quarried limestone house.

"Yep. Grandpa was smart. He made those walls three feet thick to keep us safe from tornadoes."

I felt invincible. Grandpa had thought of everything. I liked playing in the shelterbelt. It had trees to climb, the cedars made great hideouts and my brother even put in a 4-hole golf course. He sank old tin cans into the ground, took some old ball peen hammer heads, and attached them to 3-foot sticks. We'd play our brand of golf while Mom hung out the clothes.

"Don't hit those so hard," Mom warned, "when she heard one hit the side of the chicken house." Her 4-line clothesline ran along the edge of Johnnie's golf course.

"We haven't hit one yet." He said.

I saw Mom freeze with her hand still holding onto a clothespin she'd been ready to snap onto a bed sheet.

"Get in the house, now."

I'd never heard that tone from her before. We didn't argue, we just ran for the backdoor.

She dropped the sheet to the ground and followed.

"What's the hurry?" Dad asked coming in the front of the house.

"Someone shot into the shelterbelt while we were out at the clothesline."

"I saw a car slow down on the highway just a few minutes ago," Dad said, "nobody I knew. But today's the first day of pheasant season, I'll bet they're new hunters, maybe from out-of-state."

"No one with any sense would shoot into a shelterbelt. It's too close to a house."

Mom said.

"They're probably not used to the country, they saw a pheasant and got excited."

"We got scared," I added.

"I can fix that," he said.

He went to town and came back with a supply of 'No Hunting' signs.

"But what about your friends that come out to hunt?" I asked.

"If they're invited, I'll let them hunt. They know better than to shoot into a shelterbelt."

The pheasants learned to read right after Dad posted his signs.

Those multicolored birds and their mates took to strutting along the edge of our trees right along the highway—especially during hunting season.

"They know just how far to go." Mom said. "and tease worse than you kids."

"I saw one standing right under the 'No Hunting' sign," Dad said. "I think he was smiling."

Kansas got its name from the Kansa Indians. It means people of the wind.

Prairie Folklore

If Grandma caught me slacking, she'd warn I'd end up tending the County Poor Farm if I didn't straighten up. Poor Farms provided room and board in exchange for work for paupers and the disabled, but disappeared around the 1950's due to Social Security. Surviving the dustbowl and depression left its legacy.

Country Creamed Pheasant

Company will love this recipe. Serve with rice, fancy baked apples and fresh asparagus.
Serves 4 to 6

Ingredients:
- 2 2-3 pound pheasants, quartered
- ¼ cup flour
- salt and pepper to taste
- ¼ cup butter or margarine
- ¼ cup cooking oil
- 1 cup cooking sherry
- 1 cup half and half
- 3 beaten egg yolks
- ¼ cup butter or margarine
- dash nutmeg

Directions:
1. Mix flour, salt and pepper in a zipper bag. Add pheasant quarters one piece at a time. Shake.
2. In large skillet, melt butter and add oil. Brown pheasant on all sides. Add sherry, cover and simmer 45-50 minutes until tender. Remove bird. Keep warm.
3. Combine egg yolks, nutmeg and half and half. Slowly pour into skillet, stirring constantly. Cook over medium heat until thick. Do not bring to boil.
4. Serve sauce over pheasant.

Prairie Meals & Memories: Living the Golden Rural

Carolyn Hall

Sweets and Treats

Prairie Meals & Memories: Living the Golden Rural

Carolyn Hall

Chicken Feed and Wedding Cakes

Wilma's kitchen was a curious mixture of smells, sweet and putrid. She was a young widow raising 2 children on wedding cakes and egg money in the late 1950's. Her daughter, Linda, and I were friends and I was always intrigued when I'd visit. Her green two story house was tucked in behind the local grocery store. Had it been in a good sized town, her driveway could've been mistaken for the delivery entrance.

She kept her chickens behind her house near the local night owls that patronized Al's Place, the local beer joint and restaurant, the other half of the business district of town. The hens roamed a modest sized yard, kept safe from the neighborhood dogs by a six foot woven wire fence and a cantankerous Rhode Island Red rooster.

I grew up on a farm outside of town and we had chickens too. Ours had the run of a 400 acre farm and we scattered grain for them and they scratched the ground and beaked through the straw for insect delights. But Wilma had a different method for good egg production; she pampered her chickens with home cooked meals.

Locals entered her house through the kitchen door, only strangers and door to door salesmen knocked at the front door. You could see her come to the door, wiping her hands on the skirt of her gingham apron. She'd stop and peer through the café curtains, her eyes widened with a glint of recognition while an unrestrained welcome found its way through her toothy smile. Her short curly hair, blond with streaks of age, was held in check with a red bandanna.

Of course you'd have to come right in and have a seat at her kitchen table. She peppered you with conversation while bowls streaked with batter clattered as she stacked and shoved them aside to clear a place for iced tea served up in glasses with daisies painted on the side.

A mixture of aromas clouded the room. Her oven brimmed with round pans of descending sizes full of exquisite cake batter. She was the wedding cake lady for the area and her creations were works of art. But while the oven emitted the scent of fine confections, the top of her gas cook stove held the ever present 2-gallon galvanized gray bucket. It bubbled with a strange concoction that my nose wouldn't let me get close enough to investigate. She kept it on her stove and stewed it continually.

"That's my chicken's supper." She'd announce proudly when she caught me gaping at it. "They like to be cooked for too. I mix chicken feed, maize mostly and table scraps. Makes for the best eggs around, makes better cakes too." She held up her glass of tea in a toast to her extra special products.

Whether her daughter was home or not, we'd sit and visit. Wilma liked someone to talk to while she baked.

"Just don't ask me for a taste, unless it's the chicken feed you're after." She grinned as I curled up my nose. "I broke my kids of trying to sneak a taste every time I baked a wedding cake. I made them each a pan of batter, gave them a spoon and made them finish every bite. They never had a longing for cake batter again, no more eating up my profits."

If we were quiet and didn't get under foot, Linda and I got to watch her frost and partially assemble her masterpieces. Her dining room table was covered with cakes in various stages of completion. She never finished them until she got to the reception hall the day of the wedding.

"Can you believe they want me to put a water fountain in this one, it's gonna be something. I'll put one on yours when you get married someday too if you'd like."

Wilma said as she tried out the pumping ability of the new accessory. Linda and I began picking out our dream cakes from the book of photographs that were kept out of harm's way on the sideboard of the dining room.

I still remember the morning I finally got to watch her put a cake together and add all the final ropes of frosting. Her hands were like a sculptor's, fashioning roses and leaves from mounds of white icing. She gently placed tier upon tier until the cake stood four levels high. Fresh cut gardenias and daises were added between the columns and a miniature bride and groom were nestled on the top layer.

"I thought you told me you wanted a fountain?" Wilma asked as she doubled checked her notes.

"That was nearly ten years ago." I said.

"Just checking to be sure you hadn't forgotten to tell me. This one has to be just right. And you can eat as much of it as you like, that's the bride's privilege you know?"

She wiped her hands on her gingham apron and took a card from its pocket.

The sentiment of the card was touching, but not as much as her handwritten note that read, "Thanks for the friendship you've shared with my daughter and enjoy your wedding present, I baked it myself."

Prairie Superstition
Sleep on a slice of wedding cake and you'll see the face of your future husband in your dream.

Cream Mints

Olmitz weddings required a lot of work and everyone pitched in to help. These cream mints are so easy even the little sister of the bride could help with them. Make them ahead of time and freeze them for the big day. Tint to match the bride's colors and use them at her shower or they look great on the cake table at the wedding. Try different flavors such as spearmint or butter rum. You can find a variety of flavors at candy and baking supply stores or on the internet along with small decorative molds. Great for baby showers or decorating the tops of birthday cakes.
Makes 6 dozen

Ingredients:
- 1 3-ounce package of cream cheese
- 2½ cups powdered sugar
- ¼ teaspoon peppermint oil or ½-1 teaspoon peppermint extract
- food coloring
- ½ cup granulated sugar

Directions:
1. Mix cream cheese, flavoring, coloring then add powdered sugar. Knead until the consistency of play dough and the color is uniform.
2. Form into small balls and roll in sugar. Press firmly into molds, then pop out the shapes.

Rosettes

German weddings and St. Ann's bake sales had the best rosettes. They're fried but very delicate, a cross between a fine pastry and a crispy cookie. You need rosette irons to make these. Purchase sets on the internet and at cooking stores—not expensive. The irons come in many shapes like butterflies, angels, scalloped circles and stars. They're so pretty, I hang them on my wall for decoration between uses. Making rosettes takes a little practice, but they're not difficult. An extra handle for the irons comes in handy when frying.
Makes about 18-20

Ingredients:
- 2 eggs
- 1 tablespoon sugar
- ¼ teaspoon salt
- 1 cup flour
- 1 cup milk
- 1 teaspoon vanilla
- dash cloves
- dash cinnamon
- oil for frying
- *Topping:*
- ½ cup powdered sugar
- or
- ½ cup sugar
- 1 teaspoon cinnamon

Directions:
1. Pour oil to a depth of 2-3" in large skillet. Heat oil to 350°. (I like an electric skillet with a temperature dial, a constant temperature is important)
2. Whisk eggs, sugar, vanilla and salt. Add flour, spices and milk. Beat until smooth.

3. Attach handle to rosette iron, dip in hot oil to heat for two minutes (a second handle speeds up the process.) The iron needs to be the right temperature for the batter to stick to it. The first few will be practice.
4. Dip the hot iron in batter to ¼" from top of iron (rosettes won't come off if batter covers top of iron) then immediately immerse in hot oil. An iron too hot or too cold causes batter to slide off before you can fry it.
5. Fry rosette until golden, 10-30 seconds. (Rosettes may come off while cooking, use tongs to remove when browned.) Lift out iron. Use fork to gently tap or push rosette from iron. Turn upside down to drain on paper towel. Sprinkle with powdered sugar or cinnamon sugar mixture.
6. Reheat iron 1 minute and repeat the process. Stir batter occasionally to incorporate oil drops from irons.

Soft Oatmeal Cookies

Eat these fresh from the oven with a tall glass of milk, Grandma's comfort food at its finest. Makes 4 dozen

Ingredients:

- ½ cup butter
- 1 cup sugar
- 2 eggs
- 1 teaspoon vanilla
- 2 cups flour
- 2 cups oatmeal
- 1 cup cooked raisins, cooled and drained, reserving liquid
- 1 cup chopped walnuts
- 1 teaspoon cinnamon
- 1 teaspoon nutmeg
- 1 teaspoon salt
- ½ teaspoon allspice
- ½ teaspoon cloves
- 1 teaspoon soda
- 1 teaspoon baking powder
- ¼ cup raisin liquid

Directions:

1. Cream butter and sugar. Add eggs, vanilla and raisins, mix well.
2. Stir in spices and raisin liquid.
3. Add flour, baking soda, baking powder and nuts. Mix well.
4. Stir in oatmeal. Let stand for 1 hour to soften oatmeal.
5. Preheat oven to 375°. Drop heaping teaspoons on greased cookie sheets. Bake for 10 to 12 minutes.

Carolyn Hall

I loved to bake oatmeal cookies especially when I got to open a new box of oatmeal. Cups, saucers and plates came packed inside the oat flakes. Powdered laundry detergent started dish giveaways too. If Mom didn't need them, we'd add it to our hope chest.

Hope chests in our house were made from cedar and became a Midwestern dowry. Young girls started their hope chests before they gave up dolls. We crocheted doilies, embroidered t-towels, quilted bedding, collected dishes, linens, and all things necessary for a future bride to set up housekeeping. Add Prince Charming, and we had everything to complete the dream.

Kansas Tornado Cookies

These buttery morsels are a new twist on the old favorite sugar cookie, half chocolate and half vanilla. Makes 6 dozen

Ingredients:
Vanilla Dough:
- ¾ cup butter or margarine
- 1 cup brown sugar
- 1 egg
- 1 teaspoon vanilla
- 2½ cups flour
- ½ teaspoon baking powder
- pinch of salt

Chocolate Topping:
- 8 ounces chocolate almond bark, broken into pieces
- ½ cup finely chopped pecans or walnuts

Directions:
1. Cream butter, gradually add sugar, beat until light. Add egg and vanilla.
2. Mix flour, salt and baking powder together and add to first mixture. Blend well.
3. Chill dough at least 1 hour.

Chocolate Dough:
- ¾ cup butter or margarine
- 1 cup granulated sugar
- 1 egg
- 1 teaspoon vanilla

- 2¼ cups flour
- ¼ cup cocoa
- ½ teaspoon baking powder
- pinch of salt

Directions:
1. Cream butter. Gradually add sugar, beat until light. Add egg and vanilla. Mix flour, cocoa, salt and baking powder together and add to first mixture. Blend well.
2. Chill dough at least 1 hour.

Assembling Tornadoes:
1. Preheat oven to 350°.
2. Lightly dust work surface with powdered sugar. Cut each flavor of dough into ⅓ sections, then cut into ⅓ sections again. Starting with chocolate, roll one section back and forth to form a ½ inch thick rope adding more powdered sugar to surface as needed to prevent sticking. Repeat with a vanilla section. Place side by side, press lightly and roll together to form a twisted rope. Cut in 3 inch sections.
3. Place 2 inches apart on ungreased cookie sheet. Bake 10-12 minutes or until set. Cool.

Chocolate Topping:
1. Melt almond bark in microwave, about 1 minute, stir until smooth. Dip one end of cookie into the melted chocolate. Sprinkle nuts over chocolate. Cool. Store in airtight container.

Chocolate Crinkles
The powdered sugar coating 'cracks' while these bake, leaving a soft chocolate center—
a chocolate lover's dream.
Makes 4 dozen

Ingredients:
- ¾ cup cocoa
- ¼ cup butter or margarine
- 3 eggs, beaten
- 1½ cups sugar
- ½ cup cooking oil
- 2 teaspoons vanilla
- 2 cups flour
- 2 teaspoons baking powder
- ¼ cup powdered sugar

Directions:
1. In large bowl, cream butter and sugar. Blend in eggs, oil and vanilla.
2. Combine flour, cocoa, baking powder. Add to above mixture and stir until well blended. Chill 2 hours or overnight.
3. Preheat oven to 375°.
4. Put powdered sugar in small bowl. Form dough into 1" balls and roll each in powdered sugar. Place on ungreased cookie sheet 2" apart.
5. Bake 10-12 minutes or until edges are firm.

Peanut Butter Cyclones

When peanut butter and chocolate collide, it's always a special treat.
Makes 4 dozen

Ingredients:
- 1 cup butter or margarine, softened
- 1 cup packed brown sugar
- 1 cup smooth peanut butter
- 1 egg
- 1 teaspoon vanilla
- 2 cups flour
- 1 teaspoon soda
- ½ teaspoon salt

Filling:
- 1½ cup semisweet chocolate chips, melted

Directions:
1. Cream butter, peanut butter and sugar. Add egg and vanilla. Beat well. Add flour, soda and salt. Blend thoroughly. Chill until firm.
2. Preheat oven to 375°.
3. Divide dough into halves. Dust work surface with powdered sugar. Roll each section into 8x10 inch rectangle.
4. Spread each of the rectangles with half of the melted chocolate chips.
5. Starting with the longer end, roll dough as for jelly roll to form two long logs. Wrap each in waxed paper, seam side down and then wrap again in plastic wrap. Chill.
6. Cut into ¼" thick slices.
7. Bake on ungreased cookie sheet 7-10 minutes.

Almond Lace Rings

A tasty butter wafer pretty enough to serve on a fancy doily—just don't use one of Grandma's hand crocheted heirlooms. You can substitute pecans for the almonds, then there's no need to blanch the nuts.
Makes: 3 dozen

Ingredients:
- ½ cup butter or margarine
- 1 cup sugar
- 1 egg, well beaten
- 1¾ cup flour
- ¼ teaspoon salt
- 2 teaspoons baking powder
- 1 teaspoon vanilla
- ½ cup almonds, blanched and chopped fine

Topping:
- 1 tablespoon sugar
- ¼ teaspoon cinnamon
- 18 almonds, blanched and split in half

Directions:
1. Work butter until creamy. Add sugar, vanilla and egg, mix well.
2. Add flour, salt and baking powder, mix well.
3. Form into log, 2" in diameter. Roll in chopped almonds. Wrap in waxed paper and chill at least 1 hour.
4. Preheat oven to 350°.

5. Cut ¼" slices and place on cookie sheet. Mix cinnamon and sugar. Sprinkle on each cookie slice. Place 1 almond half in center of each cookie.
6. Bake 12 minutes, do not brown.

Prairie Know-How
For an oven with no thermometer, place a shallow pan of flour in the oven. If the flour turns light brown, it's just right. If it gets dark, it's too hot.

Prairie Meals & Memories: Living the Golden Rural

Graveyard Stew

Farm living in the 1950's meant self-sufficiency and sacrifice, fair weather or foul, sick or not, everyone had chores. My large extended family harvested, picked, milked, butchered and gathered most of what we consumed. Fresh chicken and guinea eggs, beef fattened on lush green pastures, crisp garden vegetables and oh yes, that repulsive raw whole cow's milk with specks of yellow cream floating on the top satisfied our hunger. Ironically, we didn't drink the milk after it went through the cream separator—the 'blue milk' or skim as it's called today wasn't thought to be for human consumption. We added supplements to it and fed it to the freshly weaned calves. That concoction smelled better than the whole milk I choked down under protest. I knew it had to taste better too.

My Grandmother Schreiber contributed her home baked bread to the family's larder. The steely eyed, lean matriarch of the family stood barely 5' 4" as she took on an enormous body of dough every Monday morning. I didn't like tangling with her or her bread and thought she felt the same way about me.

However, being the youngest and least helpful with the outside farm chores I stayed captive in the house as Grandma's helper. She was the family's head cook, housekeeper and chicken executioner. I was a probationary cook at the age of seven and could be banished from her kitchen for the slightest transgression.

Her bakery production took over the entire green Formica topped family table. A solitary frosted light fixture in the center of the ceiling dimly lit our crowded workspace. She stood, arms buried up to her elbows in bread dough, wrestling with her elastic creation and meting it out into charred bread pans. The rich warm smell of the melted butter made my mouth water while her keen eye measured every drop I slathered onto the tops of the loaves. While she looked the perfect cook in her pink flour sack apron neatly trimmed with miniature yellow rickrack, I stood covered in flour dust with grease stains trailing down my shirt and onto my dungarees. Grandma fashioned lovely aprons, but not for me.

Once I tried to sneak a piece of dough to taste by pinching off a small bit from the bottom of the huge heap on the table. Covered in velvety soft flour, it powdered my chin as I raised it to my mouth. She admonished me before I could eat it and warned that raw dough wouldn't dissolve in my stomach. Instead, it would swell to unknown proportions even a doctor might not be able to control. Remembering my grandfather Schreiber died young from undetermined stomach problems, I had no doubt she spoke from experience. This worry haunts me still.

Never one to waste leftovers, she found ways to use up every morsel of her creations. The recipe of choice was a tasty afternoon snack called Graveyard Stew. As a child, I imagined all sorts of horrors surrounding the origin of that moniker and Grandma never revealed its source. The stew consisted of stale homemade bread, generously buttered and torn into large chunks, then toasted under the gas broiler until every cell crunched. We filled our bowls with the golden brown pieces. We passed a pitcher of hot milk around the table to drench the dried bread. I grimaced at my turn with the awful fresh cow's milk, and quickly added the final ingredients to my bowl, heaping spoonfuls of cinnamon and sugar. I always snuck at least two more spoonfuls when I thought Grandma wasn't looking. The sweet spicy flavor disguised the disagreeable flavor of the raw milk and the satisfying crunch of the bread made each bite a treat.

Lucky for me the hot milk dissolved any evidence of gluttony and I carefully drank the last drop to avoid the slurry of milk and sugar from being discovered later in the kitchen sink. We each had our favorite bowl and my lime green ceramic dish always met Grandma's scrutiny. My lack of weight concerned everyone. Dad said he held my hand so the wind wouldn't blow me away. But I remained a confirmed fussy eater. Grandma had a much harsher German word for it. She'd spit it out of the back of her throat at me in her more exasperated moments.

I felt a bother to her and she was a vexation to me, much like siblings tolerating each other's presence. My friends had grandmothers they'd visit for long weekends and holidays. I so wished my grandma lived far away and I could go visit her. We'd laugh together and maybe learn to like each other, perhaps even love each other in time. Occasionally I'd go on a Grandma visit with one of my friends. Their grandmothers were lilac scented, soft, and layered in calico and skin folds.

They always greeted us with hugs and "My how you've grown" and "Aren't you just the prettiest little girl" declarations. I can't remember if Grandma ever hugged me. She was my sole surviving grandparent and I felt gypped.

Over the next few years, my mother's health took a near fatal plunge and she struggled to recover from strokes that struck first her left, then her right side. Not yet fifty, she relearned to walk and talk. Grandma's role in the household increased and my frustrations with her grew, overshadowed by my mother's crisis.

As I reached my all-knowing teen years, Grandma grew even more contrary and distant. I felt our roles reversing. She rifled through my sewing, mistaking it for hers. We battled over my homework. She insisted my books belonged to her and I had to wait my turn to use them. One role she never confused however, was that of authoritarian over me. My mother encouraged me to let it go in one ear and out the other; confrontation only escalated Grandma's agitation.

One Sunday morning in late spring, her behavior could no longer be ignored. Grandma decided to go home with the wrong family after church. Mom tried to persuade her to come home with us, and Grandma got hostile. The elderly widowed neighbor man winked at Mom and helped

Grandma into the car with his family. When we got home, his daughter called, "Your Grandmother's a bit confused," she told my sister. "She thinks my dad and she are married. We'll feed her lunch and Dad said he'd drive her home later. Is that all right?"

My family formed a protective shield around the proud gray-haired woman who still cooked and cleaned but could no longer be left alone. We listened for the familiar creaks of the well-worn wooden staircase that led up to her bedroom and intercepted her dangerous late night walks. Her energy was amazing; she kept in perpetual motion.

My older sister joined the Army and my parents took a long overdo vacation to help her relocate to Texas. At seventeen, I stayed home and took care of Grandma. During the day, I let her assume command, within reason, as my mom cautioned me. At night, I slept on the couch as guardian of the front door. With the screen door secured, one of the few door locks in our home, I could hear her rattle the handle against the lock and catch her. Once outside she'd head down the driveway toward the highway, her favorite route of escape. Until her wandering started, we never locked it. Dad secured the other outside door by placing a dresser in front of it.

I soon left for college at Kansas University, 250 miles away. Grandma died during my sophomore year. In the 1980's I began work as a dietitian in a nursing home, one of the first in the area to have a specialized Alzheimer's wing. It was there I found my grandma. The pieces of the puzzle came together and I cried my first tears for her. A combination of sorrow, regret and gratitude stirred in me. I became angry with the ignorant child in me who was callous and unforgiving. My grandma had bravely fought against a monster that slowly dragged her into the abyss of Alzheimer's and no one understood. She held her ground for years. Grandma kept what little dignity the disease would allow her by masking the symptoms and compensating. Sometimes that meant exerting the only control she could over an unsuspecting impish granddaughter.

I finally acknowledged the blessings of my Grandma, a scrappy survivor. She wasn't the doting Grandma of my dreams, but a hard-working, tenacious role model I wished I'd known better. I regret not hearing her stories. The daughter of a German immigrant, she worked full-time by the age of fourteen. She buried two of her three children, a son at the age of two from whooping cough, and a daughter in her thirties from polio. No wonder we never missed a vaccination. I swear we got every polio shot two times over, at least it felt like it. My grandpa died unexpectedly before my Mother turned 20, leaving Grandma to run the farm until my parents married years later.

How could I have missed the legacy of this incredible lady? I failed to see her determination as she fought the darkness, but I vowed to use this lesson. My goal became finding the person behind the cloud in my Alzheimer patients.

Whether destiny or luck of the job market led me to work

with the elderly—I'll never know. The unconditional love offered by the residents of the nursing home overwhelmed me, and I learned to love my grandmother through them.

When faced with patient weight loss problems, I introduced my favorite snack, Graveyard Stew. Even the fussy eaters couldn't resist the sweet and spicy treat. Grandma always knew how to get the best out of me.

Haystacks

These chocolate no-bake cookies and a glass of cold milk are a marriage made in heaven. A fast and easy recipe that makes a great learn-to-cook recipe for kids. The key to these cookies is the 1 minute boil, not more, not less.

Makes 3 dozen

Ingredients:
- 2 cups sugar
- ½ cup butter or margarine
- ¼ cup cocoa
- ½ cup milk
- pinch of salt
- ½ cup chunky peanut butter
- 2 teaspoons vanilla
- 3 cups oatmeal
- ½ cup coconut (optional)

Directions:
1. Combine sugar, butter, milk, salt and cocoa in saucepan. Stir constantly over medium heat. Start timing when the mixture reaches a rolling boil. Boil for 1 minute only. Remove from heat.
2. Add peanut butter and vanilla. Mix until peanut butter dissolves. Blend in oatmeal and coconut if desired.
3. Drop by teaspoon onto waxed paper. Cool.

Pumpkin Bars

Good anytime but a great way to use the Halloween pumpkins you didn't carve.
Makes 2 dozen

Ingredients:
- 4 eggs
- 1⅔ cups sugar
- 1 cup oil
- 2 cups cooked and pureed pumpkin or 1 16-ounce can
- 1 teaspoon salt
- 1 teaspoon baking soda
- 2 teaspoons baking powder
- 2 cups flour
- 2 teaspoons cinnamon
- ½ teaspoon pumpkin pie spice

Frosting:
- 4 ounces cream cheese
- ¼ cup margarine
- ½ teaspoon vanilla
- 1¾ cups powdered sugar

Directions:
1. Preheat oven to 350°.
2. Beat eggs, sugar, oil and pumpkin till light and fluffy.

3. Stir together flour, baking powder, spices, baking soda and salt. Add to pumpkin mixture and mix thoroughly.
4. Spread in greased 15"x10" pan. Bake 25-30 minutes. Cool. Frost.

Frosting:
Beat cream cheese and margarine until soft. Stir in vanilla. Add powdered sugar, a little at a time, beating until smooth and desired spreading consistency.

Sunflower Seed Cookies

Here's a tasty addition to an old favorite oatmeal cookie. A delightful difference you're sure to enjoy. Makes 4 dozen

Ingredients:
- 1 cup butter or margarine
- 1 cup firmly packed brown sugar
- 1 cup granulated sugar
- 2 eggs
- 1 teaspoon vanilla
- 1½ cups flour
- ½ teaspoon salt
- 1 teaspoon baking soda
- 1 teaspoon nutmeg
- 1 teaspoon cinnamon
- 3 cups quick cooking oatmeal
- 1 cup shelled, salted sunflower seeds

Directions:
1. Cream butter, sugars, eggs and vanilla. Add flour, salt, soda and spices. Blend well.
2. Stir in oatmeal and sunflower seeds.
3. Chill at least 1 hour.
4. Preheat oven to 350°. Drop by teaspoon on an ungreased cookie sheet. Bake 10 to 12 minutes.
5. Cool and store in airtight container.

Carolyn Hall

This and That

Prairie Meals & Memories: Living the Golden Rural

In Heaven There is No Beer

About twenty-five percent of Kansans can trace their heritage back to Germany. My family provides a fair amount of that number. Dad's father grew up in a small village near Bitburg, Germany known for Bitburger Pilsner, one of Germany's most popular beers since 1870.

In the late 1970's, I lived just sixty miles from Bitburg and witnessed first hand German's enjoying what my landlord called a "cool blonde", a light, gold colored beer, a pilsner style. Cool, not cold, was the rule. I made the mistake only once of serving beer from the refrigerator. After that, I kept the beer I served to our German friends in the coolest part of the basement. This explained a lot.

My Great Uncle Frank lived with my family on the farm when I grew up. He'd lost his hearing in WWI and reverted back to speaking mostly German. A longneck bottle of beer, his favorite way to slake his thirst on a dusty Kansas summer day, never saw the inside of the icebox, it came up from the root cellar—cool, not cold.

With all the heritage surrounding us, our little Kansas town of Olmitz loved to celebrate German style. Weddings were the best—an all day affair, with hundreds of guests. Lunch, a reception, dinner and lots of beer—way into the late evening at the wedding dance. I learned to Polka, do the Grand March and the Flying Dutchman, but never learned to enjoy beer. I hated the taste. Light, dark, cold or cool, I opted for a Dr. Pepper. When the band played "In Heaven There Is No Beer", the crowd sang along about the need to drink it while you're here. I always thought heaven must be wonderful because it didn't have that bitter flavored stuff.

Even though I couldn't stand to drink it, I discovered it could add a boost to my recipes.

"Seems like a waste of good beer," Dad said. But when he tasted the results, he didn't mind sacrificing a cup or two to the cause. He'd stop me however before I poured any excess I didn't need down the drain. When it's the national drink of Germany, that's a crime.

You can hoist your Pilsner in the air and I'll add to the salute with my beer bread. "Prost."

Red Beer

Whenever an out-of-town in-law joined our family, Dad initiated them at his favorite tavern by ordering them one of these. The bartender served it up in a frosted fishbowl—a 16 ounce beer goblet on a 4" pedestal. Red beer is the only way I can drink beer and halfway enjoy it. Adventuresome folk use V-8 with Worcestershire sauce or spicy V-8 instead of tomato juice. Some add a dash of pepper. To frost a beer mug, rinse it with water so it's damp and put it in the freezer for at least 30 minutes.
Serves: 1 large

Ingredients:
- 4 ounces tomato juice, chilled
- 12 ounces cold Coors or comparable pale brew (this is open to discussion)
- salt to taste

Directions:
1. Pour beer into frosted goblet—preferably minimal or no head.
2. Top off with tomato juice, add salt if desired.
3. Stir gently. Kick back and relax.

Cheesy Beer Bread

Different varieties of beer will change the character of this bread. It's worth parting with your favorite brew to stir up this hearty loaf.
Yields 1 loaf

Ingredients:
- 3 cups flour
- 2 tablespoons sugar
- 1 teaspoon salt
- 4 teaspoons baking powder
- 12 ounces beer (I prefer a dark beer)
- ½ cup grated Swiss or Asiago cheese
- ½ cup grated Parmesan cheese
- 2 tablespoons minced garlic
- 1 tablespoon chives
- 1 teaspoon basil
- 2 tablespoons butter or margarine, melted

Directions:
1. Stir flour, baking powder and salt together. Add beer, cheeses and spices, mix.
2. When dough begins to form a ball, use your hands to incorporate all the dry ingredients. Dough should be moist throughout with no dry spots.
3. Preheat oven to 375°. Place into heavily greased 8" pan, making sure dough reaches all corners. Bake 45 to 50 minutes.
4. Cool 10 minutes before removing from pan. Drizzle top with melted butter or margarine.
5. Allow another 10 minutes before slicing.

Prairie Tip
I learned to make this with self rising flour, but found that I had better luck using regular flour and baking powder added separately because I didn't use the flour often enough to keep the baking powder in it effective.

Self-rising flour has the baking powder and salt already added. It makes for quick biscuits and pancakes but is less popular with all the modern mixes.

Prairie Remedy
Flat beer will remedy an upset stomach.

Beer Bundt Cake

Serve this moist delight warm with a hot cup of coffee. You can substitute the prunes for dates. A pale ale suits this recipe best.
Serves 16

Ingredients:
- 1 cup butter or margarine
- 3 cups flour
- 1 cup chopped nuts
- 2 well beaten eggs
- 2 teaspoons soda
- ½ teaspoon cloves
- ½ teaspoon allspice
- 1 teaspoon cinnamon
- ½ teaspoon salt
- 2 cups brown sugar
- 2 cups chopped prunes
- 2 cups beer

Glaze:
- ¾ cup powdered sugar
- 1 tablespoon melted butter or margarine
- 2 tablespoons dark rum or ¼ teaspoons rum extract plus 2 tablespoons milk

Directions:
1. Preheat oven to 350°.
2. Cream butter and sugar. Add eggs and mix.
3. Combine flour, soda, salt and spices. Reserve ¼ cup.

4. Stir flour mixture into creamed ingredients.
5. Dust nuts and prunes with reserved flour mixture. Combine with above ingredients.
6. Add beer last and blend well. Pour into well greased bundt pan. Bake 1 hour and 15 minutes.
7. Remove from oven. Allow to cool 10-15 minutes. Invert pan on cake plate and gently shake to loosen cake.

Glaze:

While cake cools, mix powdered sugar, butter and rum. Stir till smooth and drizzle over warm cake. Serve warm.

Carolyn Hall

Dairy Delights

Prairie Meals & Memories: Living the Golden Rural

All We Have We Owe to Udders

On the farm, you grow into your chores and when you're the youngest you always start at the bottom—or in my case at the rear. When I was five, we still milked in the old red barn, open on the south side and heated by the warmth of the cows. Twice a day, we drove the cows into the barn and led them into the stanchions. These wooden contraptions, made from 2x4's, secured the cow's head while milking and allowed her to dine on tasty hay at the same time. Mom, Dad and my older sisters did the milking by hand while sitting on a one-legged milking stool. This took practice and talent—both the milking and the balancing on what looked like a giant letter 'T'.

Once the first round of cows stood ready to be milked, I took up my position behind the cow with the busiest tail. My job, preventing the switching pendulum from whipping someone's face, came with its' own hazards. Keeping a cocklebur-filled shaggy tail from swatting a hungry August fly or dodging an unexpected nature's call, kept me focused on the task in my hand.

Times changed and so did the farm. Dad bought electric milkers that allowed us to milk more cows in less time. This proved important as my sisters moved on to jobs and their own families. Eventually, with the help of neighbors, he built a cinder block state-of-the art dairy barn. It had three metal stanchions that held the whole cow, not just her head. Her posterior fit snuggly inside, confining her confounding tail. The cows stood in a parallel line to a concrete three-foot 'pit' which provided the perfect place to stand and attach and monitor the electric milkers. A loud, powerful pump sent the milk through stainless steel pipes into the next room, through a filter and into a refrigerated bulk milk tank.

Several times a week, the dairy company sent a refrigerated tanker truck to pick up our milk. We had to keep strict sanitary standards in the room that held the milk. The driver tested the milk for bacteria, temperature and taste, (Wild onions and wheat grass eaten at the wrong time of year caused the milk to taste bitter. We couldn't even use it to cook because it tasted so strong.) If any one of the tests weren't passed, we couldn't sell it as grade A dairy milk and it got sold to the local cheese plant for a big loss in farm revenue.

When I started high school, my mother's health kept her from the dairy barn and Dad missed the afternoon milking with his job in the oilfields. Our herd had dwindled in numbers and when my brother neared graduation and a date with the Navy, Dad decided to end our milk production. He gradually sold off the cows and kept the best until last. We still had to milk a few by hand until they sold. I'd been spoiled with the electric milkers and had to learn the art of doing it by hand.

Unfortunately for me, Slowpoke, the monster Holstein

cow stayed until we shut the barn down. She was stubborn, huge and slow, but produced the most milk of any of our herd. I got the biggest bucket we had. My pride got the best of me and I wanted to see how full I could get the bucket. After I painstakingly extracted nearly three gallons of the warm frothy liquid, she raised her big corral-muddy foot and plopped it right in the middle of the bucket. She'd fouled my twenty minute effort. I would have to pour it down the drain—or I could take my revenge. I carefully got her hoof out of the bucket without spilling much of the now brown tinged milk.

Dad rounded the corner just in time to see the remnants dripping down her head. She just chewed her cud, unmoved and unrepentant.

"Looks like you've had a little problem here." Dad said.

"Nothing I couldn't handle." I replied and opened the gate to the stanchion and watched as she dripped all the way to the door. Happily, Slowpoke's new owner picked her up before I had another chance at a full bucket of milk.

Prairie Superstition

If you scare a cow, she'll go dry (quit giving milk). This can be from a low flying Air Force Jet from the nearby training area, or a little girl that figured out if you stare intently into a cow's eyes, slowly walk up to her, stop suddenly and then jump, the cow will flinch and run. She might take the whole herd with her. Two rules of cow scaring: 1. Don't do it to the bull, 2. Don't do it when Grandma's watching, who believed this superstition.

If you stood in someone's way you might be told to "Milk it or move it."

"Were you born in a barn?" Mom's favorite response when we forgot to close the front door to the house.

Chocolate Delight Cream Pie

Thick, rich and chocolate, what more could you ask for? You can intensify the chocolate by substituting dark chocolate chips. Bury this treasure under a thick layer of meringue (recipe on page 172) or whipped topping. If you don't top with meringue, use 3 whole eggs instead of the egg yolks and egg listed below. Skim milk works fine in this recipe. Old Fashioned Pie Crust recipe on page 112.
Makes one 9" pie

Ingredients:
- 1 9" pie crust, baked and cooled
- ¾ cup sugar
- ⅓ cup cocoa powder
- ⅓ cup cornstarch
- ¼ teaspoon salt
- 4 egg yolks, plus one whole egg, beaten
- 3 cups milk
- ¾ cup semi-sweet chocolate chips
- 3 tablespoons butter or margarine
- 1 tablespoon vanilla

Directions:
1. In saucepan, add sugar, cocoa, cornstarch and salt. Stir until well blended.
2. Combine eggs and milk. Gradually pour into dry ingredients. Whisk constantly over medium heat.
3. Cook until mixture just comes to boil. Remove from heat.
4. Stir in chocolate chips, butter and vanilla until melted and well blended.
5. Pour into crust. Top with meringue. Follow instructions for baking meringue. Chill 4 hours before serving.

Blueberry Ice Cream

There's nothing like homemade ice cream, especially when someone else turns the crank. You can substitute different berries or peaches for the blueberries. Serve by itself or with peach cobbler. Makes 1 gallon.

Ingredients:

- 1 quart milk
- 2 cups sugar
- ¼ cup flour
- ½ teaspoon salt
- 4 eggs, slightly beaten
- 1 tablespoon vanilla
- 1 quart light cream
- 1 can sweetened condensed milk
- 1 pound frozen blueberries, thawed and mashed

Directions:

1. Combine milk, sugar, flour and salt in saucepan. Cook and stir over low heat until slightly thickened, about 15 minutes.
2. Add a small amount of hot mixture to beaten eggs, stirring constantly until well blended. Slowly add to rest of hot mixture in saucepan. Cook and stir over low heat until thick, about 2 minutes. Cool quickly in refrigerator.
3. Stir condensed milk into blueberries. Add to cooled mixture and blend in vanilla and light cream.
4. Freeze according to ice cream freezer instructions.

Lazy Day Ice Cream

The kids can make this on a long summer day and looking for a fun project. The flavor possibilities are endless but Nesbitt's ® Orange Soda and Nehi ® Grape led in popularity.
Makes 2 quarts

Ingredients:
- 4 12-ounce cans any flavor soda pop
- 2 cans sweetened condensed milk

Directions:
Pour ingredients into hand or electric freezer. Process according to instructions for your machine.

Homemade Sweetened Condensed Milk

Farmers always looked for ways to watch their pennies. You didn't make a special trip to town when you had a craving for a dessert and didn't have this necessary ingredient.

Makes about 14 ounces or 1 store-bought can

Ingredients:
- 1 cup instant non-fat milk
- 3 tablespoons butter or margarine, melted
- pinch of salt
- ⅓ cup boiling water
- ⅔ cup sugar

Directions:
1. Place all ingredients in blender. Beat until smooth.
2. Refrigerate until needed in tightly covered container

Prairie Tip
After gathering your dry clothes from the clothesline, lay them on the table one by one, sprinkle them with water, roll them up and put them in a plastic bag and store them in the freezer. On ironing day, take them out one at a time and they're ready to press.

Carolyn Hall

Hand Crafted

Prairie Meals & Memories: Living the Golden Rural

You'll Need More than Grandma's Lye Soap to Get those Knees Clean

"Mom," Clay said when I picked up the phone. "Can you give me some pointers on cows?"

That's not a question I expected to hear from my son his freshman year at KU. K-State is the agriculture college in Kansas. Besides that, he was studying engineering.

My kids hadn't had a lot of exposure to cows, except on visits to the farm. My curiosity went into overdrive.

"What exactly do you want to know?"

"A bunch of guys from the fraternity are going out Saturday night and invited me along." He said. I could here a hesitation in his voice. "They want to take me cow tipping with them. It won't hurt the cow will it?"

You never want to laugh when your offspring asks you questions so I had to swallow my giggles. "Son, you can't tip a cow."

"Mom, they've done it before, several times."

"How exactly do you plan on tipping this cow?"

"We won't go until dark. They'll be asleep and we can sneak up on them."

Growing up on the farm, I never worried about how cows slept. In all my farm adventures, I'd never deliberately gone out in the dark to find out. Nor did I remember waking them up to herd them into the corral for milking on many dark winter mornings.

"Cows can't hurt you, can they?" Clay asked. "I know a bull hurt Grandpa—but the females are fine, right? They don't bite like horses, do they?"

I'd been delinquent in passing on farm know-how. Failure reared its ugly head.

"If the cow has a calf, she could be very protective. And no, cows don't bite, but they might step on you and that's really painful." I spoke from experience. "So where are you going to find this cow?"

"One of my buddies has a girlfriend whose dad has a farm. Mom, they do this all the time."

I could hear the credibility gap in his voice—Mom versus the guys.

"What's the plan for sneaking up on Bossie?" I pressed on.

"You get down on the ground and crawl up to the cow."

This called for major ammunition. No son of mine would be duped on a farm. My country pride was at stake. I played my trump card.

"Clay, if you're going to do this, I dare you to call your grandpa first. Tell him you're going to crawl on your hands and knees in the dark in a cow pasture, going through whatever surprises the cows may have left for you. Then you're going to creep up on this 2000 pound bovine and knock her hooves over udder…"

"They're pulling a fast one aren't they?"

"Stick with me son, I know my cows."

Home Made Lye Soap

Grandma made this several times a year. My young hands did most of the stirring once the lye had been added. Today you need to wear goggles, rubber gloves, and preferably a mask to protect you from the lye vapors and burns. Don't reuse any of the cooking utensils for food once they've been used with the lye. You need to be in a well ventilated area to make the soap. Always add the lye to cold water. Now, if you'd like to try the recipe, proceed at your own risk, Grandma isn't available to help.
Makes 1 batch

Ingredients:
- 6 pounds lard, salt free
- 2½ pints water
- 1 can lye
- ½ cup powdered borax (optional)
- ½ cup ammonia (optional)
- wooden box
- old rags

Directions:
1. Melt lard. Add lye to cold water and dissolve in a large enameled pan, never use aluminum. Use a long handled wooden spoon or stick to stir.
2. Lard should be warm enough to pour in a thin stream into lye water. Add lard and stir until cool and thick. Add ammonia and borax. Stir slow and even 10-15 minutes or until well mixed. Chunks may result if not mixed thoroughly.
3. Line box with several thicknesses of rags. Pour soap mixture into box. Let cure until solid. Cut into cakes. Do not let freeze. (We had a long narrow enamel dishpan Grandma used to mix and then let the soap cure in, eliminating the need for the box.)

Prairie Tip
The whiter the lard the nicer the soap

Prairie women added their own secret ingredients to their soap, everything from citronella to kerosene.

Prairie Wisdom
Rub some of Grandma's lye soap under your fingernails, you'll soon find something better to chew on.

Depression Flower Garden

My grandma grew one of these every year and it made a great science experiment for my kids. It's also called a coal garden or a magic crystal garden. No part of this is edible and can be toxic. Kids will need adult supervision when growing this garden. Do not use a metal bowl for this. To keep crystals from 'growing' over the edge of the bowl, run a thin layer of Vaseline around the edge. Bluing can still be found in some grocery stores or ordered from the internet.

Makes 1 garden

Ingredients:
- 5 or 6 1-inch pieces of porous material such as broken brick, coal, charcoal briquettes, cement, sponge, cork, clay flower pot, lava rock, or limestone
- 1 shallow glass or plastic bowl
- bluing
- salt
- ammonia
- food coloring or ink
- water

Directions:
1. Submerge porous material in water, remove and place on glass or plastic bowl. Sprinkle with a mixture of 2 tablespoons water, 2 tablespoons salt, and 2 tablespoons bluing. Set in dry area with good air circulation.
2. Next day, sprinkle with additional 2 tablespoons salt.
3. On third day, add a mixture of 2 tablespoons salt, 2 tablespoons bluing, 2 tablespoons ammonia and 2 tablespoons water to the bottom of the bowl—do not pour on top of the material. Add a few drops

of food coloring or ink directly on each piece.
4. For continual blooming, add more bluing, water and salt from time to time at the base of the garden. For best results, leave garden undisturbed.

Elderly women used bluing to rinse the 'yellow' out of their white hair.

Cinnamon Ornaments

These are great for Christmas or other seasonal ornaments. They keep the aroma long after the holiday. Once dry, embellish with beads, miniature stars or small buttons. The cookie cutters that leave design imprints in the dough work well. These can become keepsakes. Do not eat them.
Makes twelve to fifteen ornaments

Ingredients:
- 1cup+2 tablespoons cinnamon
- ¾ cup applesauce
- ribbon, colored string or yarn
- drinking straw, small size

Directions:
1. Preheat oven to 200°. Add cinnamon and applesauce to bowl. Work with hands to form smooth dough.
2. Roll out ¼ of the dough at a time between two sheets of waxed paper to about ¼"-⅓" thickness. Peel off top sheet of paper and cut into desired shapes. Cut hole in top of ornament with a drinking straw. Place on cookie sheet.
3. Bake 2½ hours. Cool on wire rack. (Ornaments can be dried at room temperature. Place on baking sheet. Let stand 2-5 days depending on humidity. Turn occasionally.)
4. Thread ribbon, string or yarn through hole and tie to make a hanging loop.
5. Decorate as desired.

Prairie Folklore
Keep hedge apples also known as Ozark oranges in corners of the house to repel crawling insects.

Play Clay

When you lived a long way from town, you learned to make things out of your pantry supplies, not all of them for meals. Keeping little hands busy meant special recipes like this one. Alum can be found in spice section at the grocery store.

Makes 1 batch

Ingredients:
- 5 cups flour
- 1 cup salt
- 2 tablespoons alum
- 4 cups boiling water
- 6 tablespoons vegetable oil
- food coloring

Directions:
1. Mix flour, salt, and alum in large bowl.
2. Add 4 cups boiling water, 6 tablespoons vegetable oil and a few drops of food coloring to reach desired shade. Knead to form clay.
3. Store at room temperature in an airtight container.

Carolyn Hall

Alum is used in food to make baking powder and to keep pickles crisp. Mom kept plenty on hand to can her dill and bread and butter pickles. When I asked my big sister what it tasted like, she said, "Try it, you might like it." It felt as if my cheeks and lips would suck together so tight, I thought I'd be permanently puckered. It's one of those things you only do once, like hiding a rotten egg inside the snowball you hit your brother with.

Machs Gut!!
(Make It Good)

Prairie Meals & Memories: Living the Golden Rural

Carolyn Hall

If you enjoyed *Prairie Meals and Memories*, you'll surely enjoy
Homegrown in the Ozarks: Mountain Meals and Memories

Available online at www.goldmindspub.com